at Fight Night

at Fight Night

Tools, Techniques, Tactics, and Training for Combat in Low Light and Darkness

Andy Stanford

Paladin Press • Boulder, Colorado

Foreword by Michael Harries

Also by Andy Stanford:

Fighting with Firearms: Combat Handgun, Shotgun, and
    Rifle Skills for the Real World (video)

*Fight at Night: Tools, Techniques, Tactics, and Training
for Combat in Low Light and Darkness*
by Andy Stanford

Copyright © 1999 by Andy Stanford

ISBN 1-1-58160-026-7
Printed in the United States of America

Published by Paladin Press, a division of
Paladin Enterprises, Inc., P.O. Box 1307,
Boulder, Colorado 80306, USA.
(303) 443-7250

Direct inquiries and/or orders to the above address.

Cover photo by Ichiro Nagata, PDC.

Visit our Web site at www.paladin-press.com

TABLE OF CONTENTS

FOREWORD

I'VE KNOWN ANDY STANFORD for quite a long time—ever since 1977 when his father drove him 100 miles down to my range for shooting lessons when he was only 15 years old. I can take credit for giving him his early shooting fundamentals and guidance, but I know he has worked long and hard over the years to increase his own knowledge and to substantially improve his techniques, both in shooting and related fields.

I have seen him grow from an excitable youngster, with much raw talent, into a more thoughtful and disciplined adult. Yet he has retained much of the energy and enthusiasm of youth, channeling it for study and research. His enthusiasm in general has driven him to seek out and study many different techniques, and his raw talent, now much more refined, has allowed him to master many of the variations in the twin fields of shooting and martial arts. His description of himself as a "master student" of many teachers is a very appropriate one.

He has received "E" tickets (i.e., expert certificates) in rifle, pistol, and shotgun from "Orange Gunsite" (under Jeff Cooper) and attended quite a few diverse schools, including The Smith & Wesson Academy for low-light shooting, the Yavapai Firearms Academy (Louis Awerbuck) for Shotgun and indoor tactics, the Rogers Academy, H&K's Submachine course, Clint Smith's Counter-Sniper course, The Lethal Force Institute (Massad Ayoob), Combative Concepts, the Sure-Fire Institute, and the MYLARTE Law Enforcement Low Light Instructors Course, which we attended together. A certified police defensive tactics instructor, Andy has studied with Phil Messina (Modern Warrior), Gary Klugeiwicz (Active Countermeasures) James Keating (COMTECH), and many others in a variety of hand-to-hand martial arts and edged weapons.

Andy's "competition" background runs from the old Southwest Pistol League (with a "most improved" SWPL shooter award as a teenager) to numerous high finishes in SWPL and early IPSC nationals. He has placed well up in several of the *Soldier of Fortune* (SOF) 3-Gun matches over the years, including a 4th overall at a regional SOF event. In the 1994 National Tactical Invitational (NTI) held at Gunsite Ranch, Andy earned the coveted title of "shotist" (1st overall) and then in 1998 backed it up with a 2nd at the NTI in Harrisburg, PA, as well as another 1st place as an individual in the Ohio Tactical Officers Association 4-weapons "Top Gun" event. These are just some of the highlights of his many contest finishes.

Andy was a founding member of the SCTC (Southern California Tactical Combat) program, started by Vietnam-era Marine sniper Don Rizer and myself back in 1981. The SCTC continues to this day to put on very practical and tactically oriented rifle and pistol "events" (as opposed to competitive matches). Our allies in this endeavor have always been the Bakersfield Boys (Michael Horne and Lyle Wyatt), who have been the key people behind the SOF matches for many years. Andy participated when he was running his own shooting program in California, putting on some good events, and doing what we fully expected of all our SCTC program participants, which was to experiment freely with any type of tactics and techniques and then join in on the discussions (both before, during, and after) of ways of learning how to shoot better, not just "score" well and win trophies. Having a research and development program like the SCTC program is a great value to anyone who is trying to find out what works and what doesn't without being too encumbered by competition rules. Andy made his contributions to the program and, I'm sure, learned many lessons, as we all have and still do.

Andy wrote several articles for the *Marine Corps Gazette* in the early 1990s, and he also taught at Marine Corps Base Camp Pendleton. He and retired Marine Maj. Richard Jeppesen got together to form the Military Marksmanship Education Foundation (MMEF) in an effort to bring some improved training to the military in general and the Marine Corps in particular. He pressed me into service as the "private sector liaison" of the MMEF, since I taught at "Orange Gunsite" and was a former Marine myself. We made a good effort at passing on sound ideas and techniques, and I would like to think that we did make a difference.

Andy and I have had many discussions over the years about teaching—a separate study that is divorced from shooting ability because sometimes a great shot (or fine competitor) cannot communicate his skills to his students, and those skills are, in effect, lost to the future generations. Andy has indeed made great strides in his teaching abilities, and I would rank him well above some of those teachers who are more well known and have a larger reputation than he does. He currently conducts armed and unarmed tactical training both through his own business, Options for Personal Security, and as an adjunct firearms and defensive tactics instructor at a South Florida Criminal Justice Academy.

Lest you think I'm giving you a candy-coated version of his abilities, I will say that over the years Andy and I have had differences of opinion on how to get the job done, in terms of the exact value of certain equipment or techniques (except that it seems that we are always in "lock-step" on Laser Products flashlights). Nonetheless, sometimes good, honest men can disagree on the exact method of doing things, as long as the end result is satisfactory. Neither one is necessarily right or wrong; they just hold different opinions on particular points.

My best compliment for Andy is to say that if I received a contract to go into Hell and kill the Devil, he would be one of those people I would ask to come along and bring all their gear.

In keeping with its title, this book offers a very good overview of the entire field of low-light combat. Although some of the data is available from a variety of other sources, Andy has done a good job of pulling all of it together (even if you do get more information about the workings of an eye than most first-year medical students!). Of particular value to those who may be just getting started in any related field, he presents a number of pros and cons to help you evaluate different equipment and tactics, and he makes a point of reminding you to THINK about what you are doing in any application of force. And for those of you who are professionals already working in any field that requires much more than just a "casual knowledge" of operating at night or in low light, this book will make a valuable and logical addition to your technical library.

In my own technical library I have loaner copies of certain books that I issue to my students and friends in order to bring them up to speed on certain subjects, and then we discuss the information at their next lesson. I look forward to including two copies of this book in my technical library— one personal copy and one to serve as a loaner.

—Michael Harries
Los Angeles, California, 1998

Michael Harries is a former Marine Corps infantry NCO, Gunsite/API instructor under Jeff Cooper, and champion combat pistol shooter, praised by Lethal Force Institute Director Massad Ayoob as "a pioneer in gunfight training." The Harries flashlight/pistol technique is used by armed professionals around the world, and Michael continues to contribute to the field as a trainer and writer.

ACKNOWLEDGMENTS

SINCERE THANKS TO THE FOLLOWING:

Optometrist and reserve police officer Dr. Paul Michel, without whom Chapter 1 would not have been possible.

Bill Grube and Rich Urich of Excalibur Enterprises (aka Night Vision Equipment Corporation), John Peterson of Smith and Wesson Academy, and Lt. Col. David Lutz, USMC (ret.), for their input on night vision equipment.

Dr. John Matthews and Dr. Peter Hauk of Laser Products—makers of the unsurpassed Sure-Fire line of flashlights—who taught me much about modern flashlight and laser technology.

Michael Harries (Gunsite/API), Massad Ayoob (Lethal Force Institute), Louis Awerbuck (Yavapai Firearms Academy), Bill Rogers (Rogers Institute of Advanced Weaponcraft), Ron Avery (The Practical Shooting Academy), John Farnam (Defense Training, International), Greg

Hamilton (Insights Training Center), Bert DuVernay (Smith and Wesson Academy), Steve Moses (Southwest Defensive Shooting Institute), and Tom Aveni (also with S&W) for training in a variety of techniques with flashlight and firearm.

Ken Good, Dave Maynard, Jerry Head, Brooke Smith, and Barry Duek of Sure-Fire Institute and Combative Concepts, Incorporated, and Mike Sneen of Thor International (formerly of CCI) for sharing their pioneering work in the fields of low-light tactics and force-on-force training.

Sgts. David Paul (Philadelphia, PA, Police Department) and Mario Martinez (Hillsborough County, FL, Sheriff's Office) of MYLARTE Law Enforcement Institute for their excellent low-light class.

Bob Taylor, Greg Walker, Vince Anthony, Michael Janich, Ken Hackathorn, Adam Martin, Max Joseph, Paul Britt, and Dr. U Maung Gyi for their thoughts on low-light combat.

M.G.—whose name I must omit due to his profession—for the concept of the use of light continuum.

Reed Knight of Knight's Armaments Corporation for sharing his high-tech hardware.

My mentors Michael Harries, Lyle Wyatt, and Michael Horne—plus all my other teachers in the armed and unarmed fighting arts—for a unique and practical long-term education in a variety of combative skills. In the words of "Uncle Bill" DeThouars: I prefer to think of myself not as a Master, but rather as a Master Student of my many teachers.

Publishers Development Corporation editors Cameron Hopkins, Scott Farrell, and Lisa Parsons for the use of material previously published in *American Handgunner*, *Guns*, and the *PDC Combat Annuals*.

Col. Bob Brown, USAR (ret.), Dwight Swift, and Marty Kufus for the use of excerpts from my *Soldier of Fortune* cover story on Combative Concepts, Inc.

Jon Ford, Karen Pochert, and Fran Milner of Paladin Press for their hard work, patience, and encouragement with regard to this project.

Dr. John Matthews, Bob Taylor, Dr. Paul Michel, Michael

ACKNOWLEDGMENTS

Janich, Rich Urich, Bill Grube, and Tom Aveni for reviewing and editing my first drafts, and Richard Morey, and Paula Garber for proofreading the final ones.

Clay Babcock, Ichiro Nagata, J.C. Ponce, and all the rest for the excellent photography.

Doug Miyatake, my good friend and business partner, for the many conversations that helped to refine my ideas on these matters.

And, of course, my family for their support of my career as an armed and unarmed self-defense and tactical trainer and free-lance writer.

INTRODUCTION

THE SUN IS A MASS OF incandescent gas, a gigantic nuclear furnace. The light it provides facilitates all manner of human activity, including conflict between individuals and groups. As a corollary, inhabitants on the shadow side of the planet suffer a degradation in their ability to accomplish even routine actions. The 19th century Austrian military theorist Von Clausewitz would call this negative effect "friction," and he notes its often decisive effect on the outcome of battles.

Unfortunately, nightfall may increase the likelihood of a fight even as your ability to perform the required combative tasks deteriorates. In particular, the probability of criminal assault against private citizens and civilian law enforcement personnel increases when the sun goes down. Likewise, troops manning a perimeter can anticipate probes, infiltrations, and full-scale night assaults.

Gaining the upper hand to survive and prevail in such situations is the topic of this book. The scenarios in question

1

include not only nighttime confrontations in outdoor environments, but also engagements in the reduced ambient illumination typical of the interiors of structures, vessels, and vehicles (in short, all places and times in which the ability to see is degraded by a lack of photons).

As the subtitle states, the specific subject at hand comprises an examination of equipment and methods for combat in low light. The options presented can benefit both individuals and small units. In fact, once you understand how to fight at night, you can actually turn darkness from a liability into an advantage. But before considering any of the possible solutions discussed herein, you must first clearly define the particular problem you face. The range of acceptable and lawful actions you may take will vary with the job at hand.

Specifically, the mission of the armed forces usually contrasts starkly with the goal of civilians, the latter to include law enforcement officers. The military is tasked primarily with killing people and breaking things. Casualties, including fratricide and the deaths of noncombatants, are unfortunate but grudgingly accepted by-products of warfare. On the other hand, any deaths that occur in police work or personal self-defense are viewed far more seriously.

Hence, the means employed should follow directly from the desired end. For example, cops are duty-bound to confront certain situations head on. In contrast, the private citizen can and should retreat from potentially dangerous encounters whenever possible. If you belong to the latter group, always remember that your number-one option for personal security is a commitment to avoidance, deterrence, and de-escalation.

For that matter, even combat infantrymen and police personnel will often benefit from seeking a solution other than direct combat. To quote the Chinese military philosopher Sun Tzu, "To win one hundred victories in one hundred battles is not the acme of skill. To subdue the enemy without fighting is the acme of skill." Fighting is a brutal business, and once the Pandora's box of physical violence has been opened, the results are generally unpredictable to some degree.

INTRODUCTION

Some common approaches used to achieve military objectives in the dark are beyond the scope of this writing—for example, on-call artillery (both "star shell" illumination and various forms of warshot), minefields, booby traps, hand grenades, and final protective fires by crew-served automatic weapons, and the "mad minute" fusilade of hand-held small arms. Not that these aren't important to the soldier, sailor, airman, or Marine; they just are not addressed here.

That said, the included material nonetheless has relevance for professional warriors of any ilk, particularly in today's climate of deploying troops for peacekeeping and similar operations other than war. As always, the specific situation and rules of engagement will determine the tools, techniques, and tactics that are employed.

In any case, be aware that in a life-and-death confrontation YOU, not me, will face the physical and legal ramifications of your actions. Potential results of a violent encounter include death, crippling injury, incarceration, psychological trauma, and financial ruin (from civil lawsuits and legal fees). For better or worse, combat is perhaps the ultimate test of personal decision making.

Ergo, if something in this book doesn't work for you or doesn't apply to your circumstances, don't use it. Find something else that will achieve the same goal. Don't be limited by what is here; instead, use it as a starting point for further study, a foundation for future education and training. And always let common sense guide the choices you make.

Lastly, remember—though the odds can be stacked in your favor, no tool, tactic, or technique can guarantee survival in a lethal-force encounter. In the words of one of my mentors, "It's like chicken shit: you can choose the brown part or the white part, but it's still all shit." May what follows assist you in the event that—despite your best efforts to the contrary—it's dark and you find yourself in up to your neck.

—Andy Stanford
OPS, Sebring, Florida

3

1

HUMAN FACTORS

THE DELETERIOUS IMPACT of low light levels on a person's ability to fight stems from traits inherent in all human beings. Some mammals—e.g., the bat, cat, dolphin, and dog—are endowed by nature with physical capabilities that enhance their ability to function during periods of darkness. Homo sapiens can claim no such special biological advantage.

This is not to say that people become completely defenseless when the lights go out, but rather that, for reasons of physiology and socialization, our species does better in a well-lit environment. Fortunately, the scientists and inventors among us have devoted their efforts to ensuring that we have the technology to overcome these handicaps to a marked degree. Still, no currently manufactured implement can completely negate the effects of reduced illumination.

This chapter will examine some of the more significant physiological and psychological impacts of darkness and low light on an individual. Foremost among these is the impact on vision. Our species depends primarily on eyesight for sensory input, estimated at 80 percent of the total data processed by the brain. Without augmentation by some man-made device, the human sense of sight suffers mightily when light levels drop below a certain point. To understand why, we first need to know a little bit about how the eye works.

THE EYE

In simplest terms, the first stage of vision occurs when the retina—a light-sensitive region located at the back of the eye, somewhat analogous to the film in a camera—is struck by photons passing through the lens of the eye via the pupil. The brain then processes this raw data to create a mental image of the scene viewed.

The retina is made up of two types of neuroreceptors: rods and cones. Both types of cells are found in the retina, but the cones are located primarily in the center (fovea), and rods predominate in the periphery. Both rods and cones are photoreceptors, specialized neurons that fire when a given level of light strikes the cell in question.

With sufficient illumination, the image entering the eye can be processed by the cones; these cells give us our depth perception, color discrimination, and ability to see fine detail. This is called photopic vision. Only the very middle of the fovea can provide 20/20 eyesight; just 5 degrees off center the neurological limit is 20/70.

In low light, the rods take over. Rods provide peripheral vision, which is excellent at picking up motion—these cells serve to detect potential threats, not identify them—but they cannot see detail, depth, or color. Hence, the ability to obtain visual information is severely degraded in low light. Scotopic vision uses rods only, and the combination of photopic and sco-topic is called mesopic (moonlit night sky or the equivalent). Table 1 (p. 7) relates light levels to human vision.

The negative effect of low light on vision is most pro-nounced when going from a well lit environment into a much darker one. You've undoubtedly experienced this phe-

LIGHT LEVEL (LUX)	EXAMPLE LIGHT SOURCE	VISION TYPE	VISION CHARACTERISTICS
1,000,000	Full Sunlight	P	Discomfort
		H	Glare region, reduced form
100,000	Hazy Sunlight	O	acuity and hue discrimination
		T	
10,000		O	
	Cloudy Sunlight	P	Optimum form acuity
1,000		I	and hue discrimination
		C	
100	Electric Lighting		
10	Candlelight	M	Reduced form acuity
		E	and hue discrimination
1	Full Moon	S	Inaccurate form acuity
		O	and hue discrimination
0.1	Half Moon	P	Limit for useful form vision
0.01	Quarter Moon	I	Absence of foveal
		C	and color vision
0.001			
	Full Starlight	S	Outline perception
0.0001		C	
		O	Contrast perception
0.00001		T	
		O	
0.000001	Hazy Starlight	P	Light perception only
		I	
		C	

Table 1. Human vision as a function of light level. Data source: Gene Adcock, Armada International, 3/93.

nomenon when walking into a darkened movie theater from the lobby. Your vision at this point can typically be the equivalent of 20/800 under scotopic conditions, four times as bad as the 20/200 threshold that defines a person as legally blind under photopic conditions. This is less than 5 percent of the visual efficiency present in daylight.

The good news is that the eye will adapt somewhat to the darkness over time. The pupil will expand in seconds to let in more light, and a light-sensitive chemical called rhodopsin (also known as visual purple) will be produced on the rods, making them more responsive to low light levels.

The bad news is that this process takes a while—40 minutes for full dark adaption, not coincidentally the same duration as dusk—and is very easily destroyed. You will adapt almost instantaneously to an increase in the level of illumination. Even a relatively weak light viewed indirectly will bleach the rhodopsin in a fraction of a second.

The bottom line is that in many situations it will be fruitless to worry about letting your eyes adjust completely. For example, most law enforcement shootings occur within two minutes of arriving on the scene, when vision is still affected by vehicle lights. And even fully dark-adapted vision cannot provide the 20/20 visual acuity available in daylight, due both to the enlarged pupil (less depth of focus) and the decreased resolution of the rod cells.

After 12 minutes of dark scotopic adaption, 20/300 or 15 percent visual efficiency is obtained. Fully dark-adapted eyesight under moonlight conditions is typically equivalent to 20/180, not much better than legally blind. At a light level of 25 lux, a person cannot distinguish between a weapon and some other object in the hand of an assailant. And if the potential threat is moving, the same holds true even at much greater levels of ambient light.

Since the cones do not function in darkness, there will be a blind spot in the center of your field of vision. This is why the military often teaches "off-center" viewing as a means of seeing better at night. With practice, you can detect threats this way in extremely low light, particularly if they are moving. Perhaps of more importance, you should keep both eyes open unless you have some overriding reason not to. Binocular vision provides approximately 2 1/2 times the visual sensitivity compared with viewing with one eye closed.

The ability to dark adapt will vary with the individual and can be affected by several factors. First of all, the iris, the structure that controls the size of the pupil, contains muscles that can become less flexible with age. A high level of physical fitness will improve blood flow to the eye; conversely caffeine, nicotine, and alcohol will reduce blood

A sufficiently powerful light will cause veiling glare, which will visually disable an opponent. (Laser Products)

9

flow, impairing visual performance. Hence if you are really serious about seeing well in low light, reduce or eliminate your consumption of these drugs.

On the positive side of the ledger, there are some things you can do to maximize your dark adaption. Wear sunglasses during the day, leaving them on until just before you enter a darkened structure. Red light can be used for reading and other such tasks, since this part of the visible light spectrum affects your dark adaption the least. Finally, taking Vitamin A can help your rhodopsin production, though this is really only necessary if you suffer from an abnormal deficiency, rare in Western civilization. (And be aware that excessive Vitamin A can be toxic.)

As mentioned above, light adaption is nearly instantaneous. Extremely bright light can result in discomfort. Additionally, when the light level exceeds a certain threshold, the energy received by the rods and cones overloads the photoreceptors, resulting in a condition called veiling glare (also known as "light blindness.") When this occurs, the optic nerve is overloaded with more impulses than it is capable of handling. Clearly, it is desirable to inflict this condition on your adversary, while avoiding it yourself.

To summarize the most important points from this section: 1) the eyes will adapt somewhat to low light levels, but this process takes time; 2) the degree to which a person will dark adapt will vary between individuals, and is a function of such factors as age, health, and diet; 3) even at its best, fully dark adapted vision cannot provide the visual acuity required for positive threat identification in low light; 4) dark adaption is quickly and easily lost, so in an urban or suburban environment you may not ever be fully dark adapted. Keep these things in mind as we examine tools, techniques, and tactics.

BEHAVIORAL CONSIDERATIONS

Many other effects follow logically from a decrease in sensory input. The desire to see influences actions at both the conscious and subconscious level. For instance, people tend to look above the horizon when outdoors at night in an attempt to detect objects silhouetted against the skyline. Their attention will often be drawn to any light sources, at least initially. This is sometimes called the "moth effect."

People also tend to move more slowly and cautiously in darkness, since they can't see obstacles they could trip over. This phenomenon is especially pronounced in rough terrain, on ground with a significant incline, and/or in areas with known debris or other hazards. Take this into account when timing your actions and estimating your rate of travel.

Since there is less information available in low light, decisions normally take longer than under conditions of ample illumination. Once again, the tempo of operations will be affected. Equally important, the brain will fill in missing data based on past experience or current expectations, enhancing or suppressing information as necessary. This can result in erroneous conclusions under low-light conditions, for instance seeing a gun in someone's hands when in fact they are holding an innocuous item.

People tend to rely on their ears to a much greater degree and pay more attention to sensory input other than vision when sight is impaired. Hence noise discipline becomes extremely important when stealth is required under conditions of reduced illumination. The inability to see potentially noisy debris—for example, dry twigs or leaves—makes matters worse.

At nighttime in populated environments, the ramifications of noise are exacerbated further by the fact that human activity generally decreases during the hours of darkness. Hence, there is less average baseline ambient noise to mask inadvertent and unwanted sounds. For example, a barking dog that would go unnoticed during the daytime may attract attention at night.

In many locales, the ratio of law abiding citizens to criminals changes for the worse at night. Reasons for this are many. First of all, the majority of working people sleep at night; these folks are home in bed, not out on the street. The "cloak of darkness" conceals unlawful acts, increasing the probability of success for those who would prey on others. The likelihood of witnesses getting a clear look at a perpetrator is less. Weapons can be hidden more easily, as can the preattack movements required to employ them. Low light also facilitates escape, which can be either good or bad, depending on who is doing the escaping.

The psychological effects of low light should not be underestimated. The childhood terror of monsters in the closet may no longer hold sway, but most people are affected by some degree of unease in the dark. Some of this trepidation can be traced to a logical appreciation of criminal or enemy patterns of behavior. And still other fears may be hard-wired into the human brain from the days when sabertoothed tigers roamed the night.

The latter feelings of dread result from the collective unconscious: the experience of our ancestors passed on via genes and chromosomes. Only 100 years ago, most people still relied on some form of fire (e.g., gaslight, candles, etc.) for their illumination. Hence, in evolutionary terms the ability to control significant amounts of artificial lighting easily is a relatively recent phenomenon.

The first step to true low-light proficiency is to gain an increased level of comfort with respect to operating in the dark. Otherwise, your concentration may suffer unacceptably, and you will be overly susceptible to detrimental reactions such as unintentional weapon discharge due to startle. Darkness must become a familiar environment, as opposed to the alien and presumably hostile world most people perceive.

In general, the most important factor in a life-or-death situation is mind-set—a collection of attitudes and attributes that include, among other things, your fighting spirit (killer instinct, survival drive, heart, etc.). Confidence is a key component in any confrontation. Hence, unreasoning fear of the dark can create yet one more adversary, inhibiting your ability to perform aggressively when required.

Speaking of fear, the adrenaline dump that occurs as a result of the human fight-or-flight response dilates the pupils to let in the maximum amount of light. As noted above, the larger the pupil, the poorer the visual acuity. (Artificially dilating the pupil will typically turn 20/20 vision into 20/40 under photopic conditions.) This can make a bad situation worse, since it is already hard enough to see detail in poor illumination.

Despite these handicaps, the legal standard that applies to employing deadly force remains the same in civilian law enforcement and self-defense situations. Free-fire zones may be acceptable for nighttime engagements in certain military scenarios, but this approach is totally out of the question in a domestic affray. Spraying rounds into your living room to prevent the theft of your TV is both irresponsible and illegal.

Private citizens may use deadly force only to counter—in the words of firearms trainer and expert witness Massad Ayoob—"an immediate and otherwise unavoidable threat of death or grave bodily injury to an innocent person." In low light the primary tasks of finding, identifying, evaluating, and engaging potential threats are greatly complicated by all of the physiological and psychological factors above.

If you don't want to end up in jail—or worse, kill or maim a loved one or team member by mistake—you simply must positively identify the person whom you are engaging. Jeff Cooper's Firearm Safety Rule Four states: "Be sure of your target and what is beyond it." At night, this poses a special challenge, due both to the inability to see and the increased potential for panic.

CONQUERING DARKNESS

As a tool-bearing species, Homo sapiens has always applied brain power to the challenge of fighting in low light. Whereas other animals have to function within the inherent limitations of their physical characteristics—vision, coloration, size—our ancestors learned to produce and apply tools to increase their odds of survival.

Fire was the first medium employed by primitive peoples in an attempt to mitigate the effects of nighttime and to deter the prehistoric predators that took advantage of the darkness. The heat and light provided by the flame from a burning branch or log served as both illumination and a defensive weapon.

In fact, until the use of electricity in the late 19th century, some form of combustible material—ranging from slow-burning candles to highly volatile pyrotechnics—comprised the most advanced artificial means of countering a lack of ambient light. Lanterns, torches, and "the rockets' red glare" were all common on the nighttime battlefields of the past. Though different in some respects, all of these things were nonetheless direct descendants of the prehistoric campfire.

Today, the armed professional or private citizen wishing to prevail in the dark against a lethal opponent has a much wider range of options. Whether it be the latest high-technology night vision systems or relatively simple hand-held flashlights, each device has attributes that must be understood in order to optimize its selection and employment. Used appropriately, these implements can provide you with a significant tactical advantage over an adversary. Misused, they can often make a bad situation worse.

To avoid potential pitfalls, those engaged in low-light conflict need a firm foundation of knowledge about equipment that can augment a firearm in low light. In particular, they must have a firm understanding of how a particular piece of gear can be applied in real world scenarios. Towards this end, the next four chapters will address the subject of low-light tools in the context of interpersonal confrontations.

chapter
2
NIGHT VISION EQUIPMENT

NIGHT VISION EQUIPMENT (NVE) is undoubtedly the most impressive category of low-light fighting hardware available today. A scene that was previously invisible to the unaided eye appears as if viewed at high noon, albeit in shades of green. The latest systems allow an operator to see others clearly while remaining masked by darkness, within the limitations of the lighting conditions and the environment.

Top-of-the-line NVE is relatively pricey, although the cost is coming down a bit. This means some modern equipment is now within the budget of police departments and upper-middle-class citizens, though whether typical civilian scenarios warrant the expense is questionable.

This chapter will assist in making you an educated consumer in the event that you decide to purchase some sort of NVE. It should also help in determining an actual need for this class of equipment, or the lack thereof. There are so many different types of NVE for sale today that sorting them

A variety of light-amplification NVE weapon-aiming hardware. Clockwise from top: Litton Viewer on M-4 carbine using Aimpoint red dot sight for sighting, U.S. Military issue AN/PVS-4 "Starlight Scope," Kigre SIMRAD piggyback mounted on conventional rifle scope on Knights Armaments Co. SR-25, DIOP NADS, another piggyback design, since discontinued. (Doug Miyatake)

all out can seem a daunting task. A good first step in understanding this category of gear is to define the task that a given system is intended to perform.

NVE CONFIGURATIONS

There are three primary types of NVE: viewers, weapon sights, and goggles. Which type is most appropriate in a given situation will depend primarily on whether you are going to use the device with a firearm or not and the engagement ranges at which the confrontation is likely to take place.

Viewers

Viewers are analogous to spotting scopes and binoculars. Most inexpensive NVE from the former Soviet Union is configured this way. The best use of a night vision viewer is for surveillance, reconnaissance, or navigation; using a firearm with one is difficult at best. If you intend to employ your NVE with a gun, you'll generally need one of the next two types.

Weapon Sight NVE

A night vision weapon sight can simply be thought of as a rifle scope for use in the dark. The sight can either be a dedicated nighttime unit, an integrated day/night model, or a separate device that augments a standard telescopic sight. The advantage to the latter two categories is that they do not require that the weapon be rezeroed when converting from day to night use.

Since the device is mounted directly to a firearm and aimed along the boreline, weapon sight NVE is best suited for static roles, including night defensive positions, containment perimeters, or ambush/sniping applications. It helps if the enemy is channelized by terrain features or structural "fatal funnels." If you must move from one location to another, an NVE weapon sight can be used to scout the terrain ahead. Use the same eye to look through the device each time, and you will preserve much of your dark adaption on the opposite side.

Night Vision Goggles

Night vision goggles (NVGs) are worn on the head via a harness or helmet mount and thus provide hands-free operation. Using a weapon while wearing NVGs requires some sort of aiming device besides iron sights, most commonly a visible or IR laser. Red dot scopes such as the Aimpoint can also be used to aim a weapon with NVGs. (Each of these sighting systems is discussed in the next chapter.)

Because they automatically look where the eyes are pointed, NVGs provide increased situational awareness in comparison with using a night-vision weapon sight. Additionally, with practice you can walk across moderately rough terrain while wearing NVGs without stumbling, and you can use relative size or other cues for some degree of depth perception even with a single-tube model. For driving or piloting applications, a dual-tube model is the only way to go due to greatly increased depth perception compared with single-tube goggles.

Historically, U.S. military NVGs involve the use of both eyes, but the armed services are now purchasing night vision monoculars. With these, the eye that is not looking through the device will dark adapt largely as normal. The brain seems to integrate the two inputs fairly well, particularly if the brightness of the image on the NVE side can be adjusted to the lowest useful level. As a result, movement over broken terrain is noticeably easier than when both eyes are viewing an electronic image, and one can use conventional weapon sights, particularly red dot optics and iron sights with tritium inserts.

But no matter what type of NVE you employ, remember that you always suffer a significant degradation in the ability to perceive your environment compared with using the "naked eye" during daylight. Also, as alluded to above, you will lose dark adaption when you look into a typical night vision device due to image intensity.

GENERATIONS OF LIGHT AMPLIFICATION NVE

The generational nomenclature used with NVE (e.g., Gen II, Gen III) can be confusing. Each generation uses a different type of electronics. All of the devices discussed in this section take the available light—either visible, near infrared, or infrared—amplify it electronically, then display it on a small screen. The technological details are highly esoteric and unimportant to the average user, since all except basic maintenance must be performed by a trained technician. (Appendix B contains a glossary of NVE terms.) It is sufficient to understand the differences between generations at an effects level.

The infrared (IR) M-3 "Sniperscopes" (aka "Snooper-scopes") issued during World War II and Korea were the first

18

NVE to see widespread use, and hence represent Gen 0 night vision technology. Such weapon sights required supplemental IR illumination from a special spotlight, usually affixed to the gun along with the scope. These devices were most commonly mounted on .30-caliber M-1 carbines, due to the light weight and low recoil of that particular weapon. Bulky, fragile, and limited in range in comparison with modern night-vision systems, the Gen 0 Sniperscope nonetheless provided an advantage over an enemy not similarly equipped.

The primary disadvantage to early "active" night scopes was that, unlike more advanced "starlight scopes," they require a user-supplied source of IR illumination to work. An opponent using a similar device can see the IR spotlight as clearly as the beacon from a lighthouse. Additionally, some visible light is produced along with the IR illumination, so a strong IR source will appear as a red glow when viewed directly from close range. With spotlights using IR filters this will vary with the intensity of the light source and the IR cut-off threshold of the IR filter.

Later generations of NVE are sensitive to starlight, moonlight, or reflected light from a city or other human activity ("skyglow"). Only in complete darkness, such as inside a cave, in a darkened building with no windows, or under certain limited outdoor conditions is additional IR illumination required. In this case, the user will have to employ the NVE in conjunction with an IR flashlight or spotlight, or a conventional light with IR filter.

Gen I systems are "passive" devices, designed to amplify available ambient light electronically. The most common U.S. Gen I system encountered today is the Vietnam-era AN/PVS-2 weapon sight. The main weakness with Gen I systems—a problem with Gen 0 devices as well—is that the circuitry can be overloaded by exposure to bright light, washing out a portion or all of the image, a phenomenon known as "blooming." In earlier systems this can result in permanent tube damage. Also, the AN/PVS-2 is a fairly large piece of hardware, one that significantly affects the handling characteristics of the weapon mounting it. Finally, earlier generations of NVE suffer from edge distortion around the image, and tube life is much shorter.

Gen II and Gen III intensifier tubes are quite a bit smaller than those used with earlier generations of NVE; therefore, the overall size of the devices is more compact. Almost all of these later systems feature some sort of sophisticated protection against high light levels. This circuitry usually includes both automatic gain control and/or a sensor that detects high light levels and shuts the NVE down. Blooming is not an issue, although exposure to a bright light for a sustained period can still damage the gear.

Due to differences in the photocathode (tube) technology used, Gen III devices are more sensitive to near-IR frequencies of light common to the night sky than Gen II models, which operate primarily in the visible region of the spectrum. This is why many systems intended for law-enforcement use are Gen II, which responds primarily to low levels of visible light, such as that found in populated areas.

The latest Gen III tubes have approximately twice the tube life as Gen II tubes (10,000 hours vs. 6,000 hours) and offer better resolution. Given that the average use of a night-vision device is less than 100 hours a year, the difference in tube life is generally not an issue. There is also a Gen II+ technology that offers the high resolution and higher photocathode response of Gen III at the wavelengths typical of Gen II. As with Gen II NVE, a Gen II+ device works best under fairly bright conditions—e.g., in or near a populated area or in a rural area on a moonlit night, particularly in light, sandy terrain or with snow on the ground.

The latest and greatest in photocathodes is the Gen III "ultra" tube, which must meet a number of strict criteria, including 1,500 photocathode response, 19.5:1 signal-to-noise ratio, and 64 line pairs per inch minimum resolution. The latest MIL-SPEC AN/PVS-7D night vision goggles employ this technology. The bottom line is greater sensitivity in near IR, enhanced threat discrimination, and a much cleaner picture.

Author wearing AN/PVS-7B night vision goggles with M-4 carbine equipped with Aimpoint red dot sight, Sure-Fire light, and AN/PAQ-4C infrared laser aimer. (Ichiro Nagata, PDC)

Current U.S. military issue, man-portable, light-amplification NVE includes the AN/PVS-4 (Gen II), AN/TVS-5 (Gen II), Kigre SIMRAD (Gen II or III), and AN/PVS-10 (Gen III) weapon sights—slated to be replaced with a thermal imaging system in the future—plus the Gen III dual tube AN/AVS-6 Aviator's Night Vision Imaging System (ANVIS), single tube AN/PVS-7B/D NVGs, and AN/PVS-14 monoculars. Some older dual tube Gen II AN/PVS-5C NVGs are still in use with reserve units, and this system is pretty good, if not quite up to Gen III under true starlight only. (Note: The U.S. military is upgrading many of the above-listed Gen II systems to Gen III as the tubes wear out.)

Manufacturers of tubes for U.S. Government night vision include ITT and Litton. You won't go wrong with NVE built around tubes made by either of these companies and sold by a reputable supplier. Several foreign companies such as SIM-RAD (Sweden), Pilkington (UK), Siemens Schweiz (Switzerland), Thompson (France), Marconi (Italy), and

Odelft (Netherlands) also make state-of-the-art light amplification NVE. Quick service and repair may be more of an issue with imports than domestic models.

THERMAL DEVICES

A thermal device senses the heat level of objects in its field of view in contrast to that of the surroundings, then displays the relative levels for the user as a visible light image on a TV screen. The most common scheme shows hot areas as lighter than cold areas. This is called a "white-hot" system. The advantage of this type of equipment is that it can see through smoke or fog and can see a perfectly camouflaged person or vehicle, provided there is enough temperature differential between the object viewed and the background.

Due to the sun heating the earth during the day—and the planet cooling off at night—there will be two periods of "thermal crossover" during which the object viewed blends into the background because they are the same temperature. This occurrence will affect a highly skilled operator less than a novice one, but ultimately there is nothing that can be done about this phenomenon except to use some other type of acquisition and targeting system during these times.

The military has used thermal technology for decades. Most prolific among U.S. forces are the thermal weapon sights on the M-1 main battle tank and the Forward Looking Infra Red (FLIR) devices employed by aircraft. Both ground and airborne thermal systems played a key role in Operation Desert Storm in the early 1990s. For example, much of the footage seen on television of laser-guided bombs impacting Iraqi buildings was shot through a FLIR.

Law enforcement aviation, too, has used FLIR to advantage. Mounted in a turret on the bottom of a police helicopter, this technology is well suited for tracking a fugitive at night. In a typical incident, a fleeing car thief evaded pursing officers by hiding under a plastic swimming pool; the police chopper crew could see the perpetrator clearly, and radioed

Crew-served weapon variant of U.S. Military Thermal Weapon Sight mounted on USMC M240G 7.62 machine gun. (Lt. Col. Dave Lutz, USMC, ret.)

his location to ground units who subsequently took the suspect into custody. The equipment is so sensitive that in another situation a helicopter tried in vain to direct officers on the ground to a "phantom" suspect on a roof that turned out to be the imprint from the body heat of the since-departed bad guy!

Thermal technology is just becoming practical for use with firearms. Hughes recently won the U.S. military contract to supply thermal weapon sights (TWS) in small, medium, and large versions. Even the smallest of these devices is relatively bulky compared with Gen II or III image intensification equipment and requires more electrical power to operate, since the thermal array must be cooled. Additionally, the TWS is very expensive: a typical device currently costs more than $10,000. It is also relatively fragile and is unavailable at present to other than military users.

As one would expect, the Hughes TWS is extremely sensitive to differences in relative heat levels. A friend of mine was contracted to assist in testing the small TWS variant mounted on an M-16A2 rifle. The target was a steel silhouette hung from a stand 100 meters distant. After a magazine or so had been fired, the center of the plate began to glow from bullet impact when viewed through the thermal sight.

At the low end of thermal equipment is the "Life Finder" (aka "Game Finder"). Selling for a few hundred dollars, this flashlight-size device is intended to indicate the presence and location of warm-blooded animals by sensing their body heat. In practical tests conducted by a police officer acquaintance, performance was marginal. To be fair, this is just one data point, but in any event, the Life Finder can only assist in locating people, not in identifying or targeting them.

Undoubtedly, thermal imaging technology will continue to evolve. If other types of high-tech equipment are any indication, the price may come down as a result. Some experts predict that Gen IV NVE will be a combination of thermal and image intensification, with sensor fusion technology employed to automatically integrate the two inputs in an optimal fashion. In any case, this best-of-both-worlds capability is in the future. For the time being, image intensification devices will soldier on as the only practical alternative for those who don't have Uncle Sam footing the bill.

RECOMMENDATIONS

My personal favorite NVE/weapon combination for close-range applications (i.e., 100 meters and under) is the AN/PVS-14 monocular (or the commercial ITT model 6015, identical except for the lack of manual gain control) used in conjunction with an M-4 carbine sporting an AN/PAQ-4C IR laser, augmented by a Laser Products Sure Fire WeaponLight mount with pop-open IR filter. AN/PVS-7B/D NVGs are also okay, though they do restrict your field of view more than a monocular.

Both AN/PVS-7B/D and the AN/PVS-14 include a built-in IR diode to provide supplemental active illumination where necessary—for example, indoors. The lightweight head harness features a latch that facilitates quick detachment of the

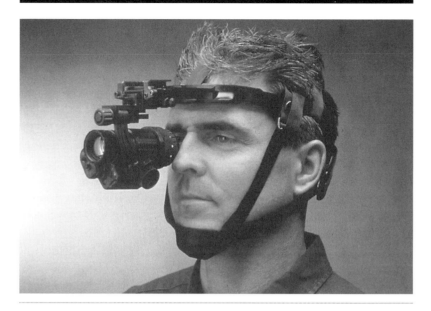

A night vision monocular such as this ITT model 6015 provides night vision in one eye while the other remains largely dark adapted. (ITT)

goggles or monocular, allowing near instantaneous transition for use of the weapon's regular sights with "white light" when desired. (With a monocular it's also possible to use the unoccluded eye for aiming.) Older AN/PVS-5Cs perform about as well as the "seven deltas" (AN/PVS-7D) for most applications, perhaps better for vehicle use, but are substantially heavier and don't have a quick-detach harness.

For a dedicated night-only weapon sight, the Raptor 4x or 6x—superior to the standard Aquila sight, currently used by various special military and civilian government teams I can't mention in print—is one of the best units around, featuring an "ultra" tube. That said, surplus AN/PVS-4 (night only) starlight scopes are still perfectly serviceable, and these can be bought for less than half the cost of the other two systems.

With convertible day/night units you don't have to reze-ro when the sun goes down. The U.S.-issue AN/PVS-10— made by Litton for the M24 sniper rifle—is probably the best

25

of the breed. Unfortunately, at a cost of more than $10,000 it's also one of the most expensive. The device simply switches between day and night settings for use in sunlight and darkness respectively.

Other options in this category include two units based around standard day scopes: the USMC-issue Kigre SIMRAD (now made by ITT), and the ITT model 7403. The SIMRAD piggybacks on top of a standard riflescope. It has a much larger objective end and hence gathers more light than the ITT 7403, which is simply a day scope convertible to night use with a special night vision eyepiece. On the other hand, the ITT 7403 is much lighter, but it's not nitrogen purged and hence prone to fogging up.

Lastly, if you want a simple viewer for surveillance applications, ITT's night enforcer 150/160 monocular and 250/260 binoculars are well thought out, rugged units with excellent human engineering. The 150 and 250 use Gen II tubes, and the 160 and 260 are Gen III. Note, however, that the tubes used in 100 and 200 series ITT NVE represent their low-end product and do not perform as well as the photocathodes used in current military issue equipment. Still, the model 150 is the cheapest modern U.S. NVE currently available, and in the past ITT has offered some attractive "easy payment" packages for police departments that wish to equip their officers with such capability.

Lately the market has been flooded with Russian NVE, and I am often asked about the quality and reliability of these units. Image resolution is usually far inferior to that of the latest U.S. NVE. Determining the actual technology generation of a given device can also be a problem. (And be warned that the advertising on this subject with equipment made in the former Soviet Union may not reflect reality.) Surplus Russian NVE inevitably does not have state-of-the-art bright source protection.

On the positive side, some of the NVE produced in the former Soviet Union is downright cheap; I've seen Russian monocular night vision viewers for sale in large discount department stores for approximately one-third the cost of similarly configured U.S. units. Image quality may be adequate for your application, particularly if you augment the device with an active IR illuminator. My recommendation is to compare different models, both American and Russian, and decide for yourself. But keep in mind that buying NVE is largely a matter of "you get what you pay for."

Before you take the plunge and pay a thousand dollars or more for NVE, research what is currently available from different manufacturers and suppliers. Many of the companies that make and/or sell this type of equipment can provide literature that covers technical details that are well beyond the scope of this writing. (Again, see Appendix B.) In particular, you should become familiar with the tube specification data sheets that characterize photocathode response, signal-to-noise ratio, resolution, and tube defects for a given tube. (In reality, tubes are as individual as people because they are still hand-crafted.) Also, note that Gen I tubes cannot be "reconditioned" to give additional service life, no matter what the seller may claim.

NVE used on operations during which counterdetection is a concern should include some means of shielding the green glow of the image reflected on the user's face. Most U.S. MILSPEC devices intended for land warfare applications meet this criteria. For instance, AN/PVS-7B/D NVGs seal positively against the face with flexible rubber eyecups, and the AN/PVS-4 and AN/TVS-5 weapon sights feature a rubber eyepiece with a diaphragm that opens only when the operator presses against it.

You should field-test any equipment you contemplate purchasing. Specifically, look through the device under simulated field conditions for an extended period—a full hour at the absolute minimum—and note any discomfort that develops. The harness (for NVGs) and rubber eye cups can be especially bothersome. It's one thing to take a quick peek and quite another to use the gear on an actual operation, very much analogous to taking a test drive around the block in a car versus sitting in the same vehicle for hours on an extended journey.

Prior to using NVE in the field, ample training and practice is critical. People equipped with NVE are at best approximately 25 percent as efficient as during the daytime. And even achieving this level of performance requires a significant degree of NVE experience. In particular, those equipped with single-tube NVG systems such as the AN/PVS-7B/D will need intensive hands-on training, since depth perception will largely depend on recognizing relational size cues. Practice should include suitable immediate action drills in case the gear goes down.

With regard to care of the equipment, treat NVE much as you would a set of expensive binoculars, and follow additional device-specific precautions and preventative maintenance. Use a sacrificial window over the lens to protect it from scratches. Whenever possible, keep the NVE from getting above 120 degrees Fahrenheit; for instance, don't leave it in direct sunlight or in the hot trunk of a car. Switch the device on at least once a month, and store the batteries separately when the device is not in use. (The cells can leak electrolyte.)

NVE employed in particularly humid or wet environments will have to be purged with nitrogen regularly, which requires specialized equipment and training. For most people this will mean sending it to an authorized service center. Lastly, realize that you may have to replace the intensifier tube eventually, since performance will diminish due to age and/or heavy use.

Can the average citizen benefit from using NVE for self-protection purposes? The answer is usually "not really," although we can all come up with exceptions. In most common home-defense situations there is simply not time to don a set of NVGs, and use of a night vision weapon sight on a shoulder weapon is not particularly practical inside the average-size single-family dwelling. (Imagine using a 4X rifle scope indoors and you'll see what I mean.)

Sure, a night vision viewer will allow you to surveil a

backyard or alleyway while remaining unseen, but motion detector lighting can provide much of the same function at a fraction of the cost while frightening away a large percentage of intruders. In any case, NVE is not a cure-all. It is best suited for military use plus certain law-enforcement applications. The bottom line is: if you're not a member of the armed forces or stakeout unit, other hardware options may provide more utility for the money.

29

3

LASER AIMERS, TRITIUM SIGHTS, AND OPTICAL SIGHTS

THE THREE TYPES OF EQUIPMENT addressed in this chapter share two common traits: each allows you to aim a firearm accurately when you can barely see, but none provides any supplemental illumination to aid in threat identification. As noted previously, the same rules for employing deadly force apply day or night, in darkness or in light. Hence, how well you shoot is only part of the problem.

That said, a means of directing accurate fire is essential for quickly terminating an aggressor's hostile actions once you have determined that a lethal response on your part is warranted. Surgical shooting that strikes a vital body part—generally the pelvic girdle, heart, or central nervous system, depending on the situation in question—will be required to maximize your odds of stopping the fight before you sustain damage.

When you can't see your standard iron sights, good hits become problematical. When it's dark many people tend to aim high in a vain attempt to see their front sight. The military has for years taught troops to place their chin on top of their service rifle buttstocks, lowering the muzzle. However, this "point shooting" does not provide the precision of visually verified fire. Historical solutions to aimed fire in low light include outlining the sights with glow-in-the-dark paint, tying a white string between the front and rear sights, and even wrapping a white rag around the muzzle of a shotgun.

Once again, technology has provided us with a better way. Laser aimers, tritium sights, and optical sights all facilitate surgical shooting. As with NVE, the relatively high-tech nature of these devices tends to preclude a dispassionate understanding of same. Myths and misconceptions abound, even among those who should know better. This chapter will provide a solid grounding in the real world utility of the equipment in question.

LASER AIMERS

Ever since Arnold Schwarzenegger asked to see "the .45 long slide with the laser sight" in the sci-fi film *The Terminator*, television and movies have provided us with an increasing exposure to weapon-mounted lasers. And just like the revolver that fires two dozen shots without reloading, the never-miss laser-sighted gun has become a permanent part of Hollywood mythology. In reality, the pros and cons of laser aiming devices are widely misunderstood, and this device is frequently overrated.

The acronym LASER stands for Light Amplification by Stimulated Emission of Radiation. In layman's terms, the laser beam is generated by causing atoms to radiate photons in sync, resulting in an intense, coherent beam (as opposed to an incandescent or fluorescent light bulb, which radiates photons randomly). Early laser sights—introduced during the 1970s using helium-neon tubes—were relatively bulky and expensive devices. Newer diode lasers have dramatically reduced both size and cost.

Placing a red laser spot on the target seems to provide

Sure-Fire laser aimer by Laser Products mounted on Heckler & Koch MP-5 9mm submachine gun, which is also equipped with a Sure-Fire tactical light fore-end. (Laser Products)

guaranteed hits. At least it works that way on the silver screen. Many gun owners have decided that they simply must have a laser aimer on one or more of their personal firearms, and the availability of inexpensive laser diodes places many models within almost everyone's budget. But before you rush out and buy one, you need to understand the exact capability a laser provides. You may decide that your money would be better spent on another option that better fits your low light needs.

To begin with, lasers cannot replace conventional weapon sights for serious self-defense purposes, for a couple of reasons. First of all, locating the red laser dot on the target is usually more time consuming than using iron or optical sights, resulting in a slower time-to-hit. And under bright ambient light and against some backgrounds the laser spot sometimes cannot be seen at all. Newer 635 nanometer (nm) lasers appear about six times brighter than older 670 nm versions, but the dot can still be hard or impossible to find in full sunlight. You generally can't predict the lighting conditions under which a defensive confrontation will occur. For these reasons a laser alone is not the best choice for the quick shooting typical of many personal protection scenarios.

Next, although often touted as low-light sighting systems, lasers do not assist with low-light target identification, a fundamental concern when shooting in darkness. Yes, you can place your shots more precisely using a laser spot you can see than using iron sights you cannot see. However, under most conditions in which you can't make out your sights, you can't see what you're shooting at either. In other words, you can shoot a tight group on an unidentified target. The legal and moral ramifications of firing at silhouettes or sounds eliminate this strategy from serious consideration.

Finally, trigger control is still the key to marksmanship, and flinching due to blast and recoil remains the major reason for poor shooting. Aiming with a laser sight does not magically force you to press the trigger smoothly, and it does not guarantee follow-through once the weapon discharges. Still, I suspect that many people who put lasers on their guns think that this will somehow automatically improve their accuracy. Sorry to break the news, but such is not the case. As a brief aside, let me note that a laser aimer can be of great help to firearms instructors, who can thereby observe exactly where the student is pointing the weapon and what happens to the point of aim once the trigger is pulled. The laser spot can also be used to track the path of the muzzle during drawstroke, to demonstrate the error that occurs due to improper sight alignment, and to monitor safe gun handling under dynamic conditions. These are, however, training as opposed to operational applications.

This is not to say that laser aimers aren't ever useful during a gunfight. For situations in which the shooter cannot use the weapon's normal sights—e.g., when wearing a gas mask or when firing from behind a ballistic shield—a laser may be the only practical alternative for designating an exact point of bullet impact. For NVE users, the best bet is an IR laser (e.g., Laser Products L-74 or military issue AN/PAQ-4) that is nearly invisible to someone without NVE. Due to the eye hazard they represent, lasers more powerful than 5 milliwatts are restricted to government users.

Next, a laser will allow the shooter to aim precisely while keeping his or her weapon in a close quarters ready position for firearm retention purposes, or when shooting from other body positions from which the normal sights cannot be used. It can also be used as a pointer, for covert (IR) or semi-covert (visible laser) low-light communication by a team leader.

Lastly, a laser may make sense for guards performing overwatch duty in a correctional facility, due to the deterrent effect of the red laser spot when placed on an offender and the fact that the officer is usually not in immediate danger. This deterrent effect has been documented in a number of street situations as well, but obviously can't be guaranteed. An adversary's resolve or lack thereof will depend on numerous variables, many beyond your control. That said, if the laser spot deters just one violent assault, it has probably just paid for itself.

On the con side of the ledger, a quality laser aimer costs several hundred dollars, money that might be better spent on training or other equipment unless you actually have a need for one. Also, if multiple team members are equipped with lasers, the "whose dot is that?" phenomenon is a distinct possibility. The Wilcox SO Smart laser addresses the latter concern with an microprocessor controlled beam offering seven different blink rates plus steady on.

If you decide a laser sight really is warranted, select one that meets the following three criteria: 1) the device must be rugged enough to stand up to field use, 2) it must hold its zero under field conditions, and 3) it must include suitable momentary switching. These requirements exclude several popular and inexpensive universal bolt-on models; the laser must be robust and mount firmly to the weapon, which means many "one size fits all" examples won't cut it. (However, universal systems that use solid scope-type mounts are okay.) If you are betting your life on a laser, it must be able take a hard knock and not fail or be jarred out of alignment.

The ability to hold zero is partly a function of the mount, and again a rugged design is desired, preferably one made specifically for the weapon in question. Holding zero is also dependent on the scheme used for the mechanical adjustments of the laser spot location. Some cheaper lasers are sighted in by two screws that torque against a metal flexure on which the laser diode is installed. This is somewhat imprecise and may allow the point of impact to shift relative to the dot due to recoil.

Others mount the front of the diode housing in a rubber "O" ring, moving the spot with screws at the rear. The Crimson Trace Lasergrip employs this scheme, using nylon bushings to lock the adjustment screws. In live-fire testing this laser didn't shift point of aim after several thousand rounds. However, holding zero can be an issue if the O-ring system is not properly designed.

The most positive way to zero a laser is to use prisms to bend the beam optically in the direction required, as is done

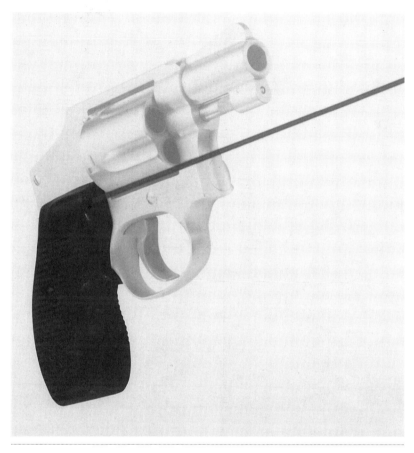

Crimson Trace Lasergrips for S&W J frame replace the stock panels.
(Crimson Trace)

by Laser Products' Sure-Fire aiming modules and the Lasermax guide rod laser. Of course, this approach is more expensive to manufacture than the other two designs but is a simple case of "you get what you pay for." Note that the Lasermax cannot be zeroed by the user at all; you're out of luck if it isn't properly aligned out of the box. (The company does guarantee bullet point of impact within 2 inches of point of aim out to 25 meters.)

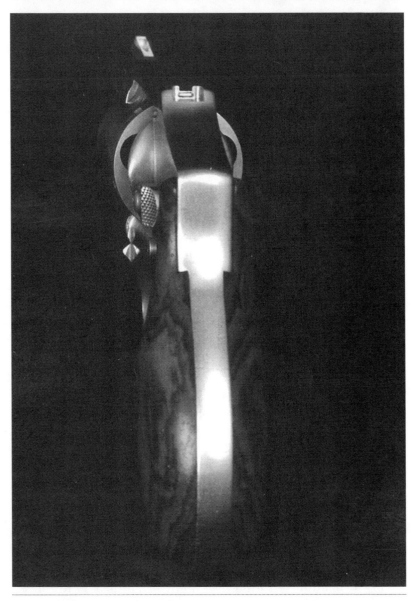

Smith & Wesson M-442 Centennial with self-luminous tritium sight inserts from Innovative Weaponry Incorporated, featuring a horizontal bar under the rear notch and a dot in the front blade. (Mike Weissberg)

When sighting in a laser aimer, remember that the beam travels in a straight line while the bullet traces an arc due to gravity. Once the two intersect, the beam will diverge farther and farther from where the projectile strikes. If your laser is mounted off to one side, it is generally best to adjust the spot so that it is offset from bullet point of impact by the same amount, then aim accordingly. For example, the Crimson Trace Lasergrip is approximately 0.5 inch to the right of the bore centerline. Of course, it's always good to keep any such offset to a minimum, mounting the laser either directly over or under the bore whenever possible.

One last point on zeroing—sighting in a laser for long-range use is a much less precise proposition than accomplishing the same end with conventional iron or optical sights. This is due both to the increasing area subtended by the beam and the fact that the spot is some distance away from the shooter. (You can mitigate the latter to some degree by simply calibrating your laser to coincide with the previously zeroed iron or optical sights.) The upshot is that a laser will not give you the pinpoint accuracy of an NVE weapon sight at extended distances. Hence the latter is better for nighttime sniping.

For tactical use, you'll want to have the ability to switch the laser on and off quickly while maintaining a normal firing grip on the weapon. Many systems (e.g., Lasermax) use a two-position on-off switch that is not conducive to intermittent use. If the laser is left on continuously, it can easily telegraph your presence to an adversary, and if there is dust, smoke, or water (i.e., rain or fog) in the air, it can also give away your location. A disable switch such as found on the Crimson Trace Lasergrip and some Laser Products modules will prevent an unintentional laser discharge.

Lastly, unless you can guarantee enough ambient light, you will need an illumination tool in addition to the laser. (Specific options are discussed in detail in the next chapter.) One advantage of the Crimson Trace Lasergrip and Lasermax handgun systems is that they leave room for a frame-mounted light such as the Sure-Fire Tactical Light. Laser Products' dual mounts for shoulder weapons accomplish the same thing in one device. If the laser is mounted to the frame in front of the trigger guard on a handgun, the only alternative for self-supplied illumination is a magazine-mounted or hand-held light, neither of which is generally an optimal approach.

TRITIUM SIGHTS

Lasers are similar in utility to another popular accessory: conventional iron sights augmented with self-luminous tritium inserts. Commonly referred to as "night sights," they are even a factory option on many firearms. Several configurations are available, the most common being three-dot (two rear on each side of the front one), rear bar underneath front dot, front dot only, and "straight-eight" (front- and rear-sight dots, which are aligned one on top of the other). The most common color for the inserts is green, with yellow, orange, and two-color versions being sold as well.

Note that many "iron" sights come with nonluminous white outlines, dots, gold beads, etc., which can enhance low light aiming but do not provide the same capability as tritium inserts.

For those who care about the technical details, tritium is a radioactive isotope of hydrogen with three times the mass of the standard hydrogen atom. For weapon sight use, the tritium is encased in a glass capsule, the inside of which is coated with phosphor particles. Beta radiation from the tritium strikes this coating, giving off light much in the manner of a nuclear powered television set. The half life of tritium is 12.33 years, and the level of radiation is insignificant from a health standpoint.

Such sights are currently manufactured by a number of companies, including Trijicon, Hesco (Meprolight), Ashley Outdoors, and Innovative Weaponry, Inc. (PT). Several gun makers offer tritium sights as an upgrade on the firearms they sell, as do custom pistolsmiths such as Bill Wilson, Richard Heinie, and Wayne Novak. Scattergun Technologies offers tritium inserts as an option on their shotgun "ghost rings," and USMC Warrant Officer Randy Allen of Weapons Training Battalion, Quantico, designed specialized front and rear sights sold by Colt for the M-16A2.

As with lasers, much of the marketing hype for tritium sights implies that they are mission essential equipment for low-light defensive situations. Yes, tritium inserts will allow precise sight alignment when it would not otherwise be possible. And there is a limited range of lighting conditions—when you can identify your target but not see standard iron sights—under which tritium inserts provide an actual advantage for surgical shooting. However, just like laser aimers, they don't help you to confirm that the person you are shooting constitutes a lethal threat in extreme low light or darkness. I know I've about beat that theme to death, but shooting blindly risks causing the same tragic results you hoped your defensive firearm would prevent.

Potential negatives to tritium sights include the chance that an adversary will see the dots from the rear and get the jump on you. On the other hand, the glowing inserts provide a means of locating your pistol in the dark—for instance, if it is sitting on a nightstand or table. Such trade-offs are very common when discussing combative hardware; you'll have to decide for yourself whether the pros outweigh the cons.

Additionally, it is theoretically possible to misalign the three dot-versions—with the front sight dot to one side or the other of the two rear sight dots. An experienced shooter should be able to tell by feel that the gun is pointed sideways, but under extreme stress anything is possible. Some manufacturers make the front dot brighter and/or a different color to reduce the likelihood of this problem, and bar-and-dot, front-dot-only, and straight-8 versions eliminate the risk completely.

Note that the recommended positioning of the glowing dots and/or bars may bear no relation to the actual vertical alignment of the sights—i.e., top of front sight level with top of rear sight. For instance, many guns with 3-dot sights will shoot high when the dots are in a row. Hence, you will need to note the relative position of the front and rear sight inserts vis-à-vis your normal daytime sight alignment, and remember to employ this aiming scheme at night.

As mentioned above, all tritium inserts have a finite useful life, but this is just an inherent characteristic of the isotope used. If you have a set, you'll need to replace them every 7 to 15 years. The reader should not mistake the preceding for a blanket condemnation of tritium inserts. They do help with surgical shooting in low light, and many of my personal firearms are so equipped. Just be aware that they are not a cure-all for night shooting situations.

OPTICAL SIGHTS

The final sighting systems discussed in this chapter comprise optical sights that place a glowing aiming mark in the shooter's field of view. This includes both battery-powered "red dot" scopes, plus more conventional telescopic sights with tritium, lamp, or diode-illuminated reticles. Each facilitates accurate shooting when there is not enough light to see conventional sights.

Red dot scopes are a reasonable approach to aiming during low-light close-quarters combat. Often used on handguns by "action shooting" competitors, they are just too bulky for serious use on a pistol or revolver—with the possible exception of home-defense applications. For this reason, any optical sight is really only practical on a shoulder weapon for use in the field or on the street.

Common examples of this type of device include the Aimpoint 5000 and Comp models, C-More Serendipity, Bushnell Holosight, ADCO Square Shooter, Tasco ProPoint, and Trijicon Advanced Combat Optical Gunsight (ACOG) reflex. The U.S. Army adopted the Comp M and ML versions of the Aimpoint after rigorous testing; the former has two night-vision-compatible settings and a lens coating that enhances transmission of IR light. The latest XD ("extreme duty") Aimpoint offers longer battery life and a brighter dot.

The Aimpoint Comp M sight has been adopted by the U.S. Special Operations Command. (Aimpoint)

Specialized units such as the army's Operational Detachment Delta have been using Aimpoints for years (see Desert Storm footage of General Schwartzkopf's bodyguards).

What do you gain by employing this type of sight? In low light applications you can see the red dot under conditions in which standard iron sights or scope reticles simply will not be visible. Additionally, in close-quarters situations a red dot scope provides the quickest possible target engagement capability—albeit by a relatively small margin when compared with "ghost ring" aperture sights and high visibility open sights during conditions under which iron sights can be clearly seen. This increase in speed is due to the fact that the target and dot appear on the same focal plane.

In my book, the primary disadvantage to a red dot scope is that it depends on batteries to generate the dot. (An exception is the Trijicon ACOG reflex, which features a tritium ret- icle for use in darkness and gathers ambient light during the daytime.) Of course, any other electric or electronic device suffers the same Achilles' heel, but it's a good idea to mini- mize the degree to which you are dependent on technology, if possible. For sure, carry extra batteries if you use this type of equipment. Delta operators tape a spare set inside the pis- tol grip of their M-4 carbines.

Some other optical sights also have features that lend themselves to low-light application. A few conventional tele- scopic sights—e.g., the Soviet PSO-1 used on the SVD Dragunov sniper rifle and the domestic U.S. Optics line— illuminate the reticle with a small internal lamp, for use at dusk and dawn. Similarly, the Trijicon ACOG can be pur- chased with a tritium-coated reticle that glows red. Or you can augment a standard scope with a high-powered illumi- nation source, such as the Sure-Fire L-120M "Leopard Light," discussed in the next chapter. Truth be told, use of visible light and a standard telescopic sight offers significant advan- tages over NVE weapon sights in many scenarios.

Even though you will always lose some light transmis- sion with a scope, a model with a large objective lens will allow you to operate under conditions in which iron sights are useless. Any hunter will confirm that an optical sight provides up to a half hour of extra visibility at dusk and dawn. The reason is that the objective end of a scope is typ- ically five or more times larger than the human pupil. Hence, even allowing for transmission losses, there is a net gain in the amount of light entering your eye.

In general, the larger the objective lens, the better. To get the most out of this "twilight effect," you'll want to optimize the exit pupil of the scope—defined as the objective dimension divided by the magnification—to match the diameter of your pupil in low light, generally between 5mm and 7mm. For best performance, any optical device should also feature coated lenses and prisms, though this will add to the cost. The best such equipment has "multi-layered coatings."

The relative low-light performance of binoculars or scopes can be calculated via the "twilight factor": the square root of the product of the magnification multiplied by the objective diameter. This will let you compare different combinations of aperture and magnification, in order to determine which provides the best balance of increased magnification and decreased brightness. For good performance at dusk and dawn, choose an optical device with a twilight factor of 17 or greater. For the same reason, choose a 30mm tube (as opposed to 1 inch) when available.

On the downside, any optical sight is inevitably less robust compared with properly designed iron sights. Hence, you'll want to have instant access to backup iron sights whenever using any optical sight, electronic or otherwise (one possible exception being the dedicated sniper).

As with lasers, you'll want to mount optical sights as solidly as possible to maintain zero under rough handling. Use two rings instead of just one wherever practical. Loc-Tite all screws and regularly check to ensure that they stay snug. Placing the scope forward of the weapon's action in a down bore "scout" configuration will allow for better peripheral vision, an important consideration day or night.

Lastly, remember: for threat acquisition, identification, and targeting you will often need to augment ambient light with self-supplied illumination. This goes for all three implements discussed in this chapter—laser aimers, tritium sights, and optical sights. Illumination is often the crux of low-light shooting problems. Which brings us to Chapter 4. The next category of equipment, while not a panacea, comes much closer to meeting all major low-light shooting requirements.

4

FLASHLIGHTS, LIGHT MOUNTS, AND SPOTLIGHTS

THOUGH NOT SO GLAMOROUS AS the high-tech devices discussed previously, hand-held flashlights and their weapon-mounted cousins are often the tool of choice for low-light confrontations. Various types of spotlights can also be useful when their size and weight are not a problem. In contrast to the expense and specialized applications of night-vision equipment—and the relatively limited benefits available from laser aimers and tritium or optical sights—a bright light provides general-purpose utility at a fairly modest cost.

The relative value of self-supplied illumination can be measured by the fact that this is the longest chapter on equipment in the book. Light facilitates target acquisition and identification, two primary goals in a violent confrontation. A high-intensity beam can also temporarily blind your assailant, increasing the odds that you will be able to dominate the situation with or without gunfire. Additionally, the light can be used to confuse and deceive. (Some guidelines on exactly how to accomplish this are found in Chapter 7.) Lastly, if you must shoot, illumination can help you do so accurately.

All this trades off to some degree against the fact that the light can give away your presence and position, but proper tactics can largely mitigate this concern. The strategy here is to change the existing lighting conditions in your favor through the use of illumination tools, while avoiding the pitfalls to the maximum extent possible via movement and timing, visually disabling your opponent, and other tactical factors. The bottom line is, though a light is somewhat of a two-edged sword, the advantages of using one often far outweigh the disadvantages.

Not all lights are created equal. In fact, some features commonly thought to be an advantage are actually detrimental. Since you are betting your life on a flashlight purchased for combat purposes, it makes sense to choose one based on an educated analysis of salient characteristics. Like the other chapters on equipment, what follows is intended to make you an informed buyer.

FLASHLIGHT GENERATIONS

As with night vision equipment, flashlights can be categorized by generation. Like analogous NVE, the earliest flashlights were significantly less capable than later models. For consistency with night vision, I classify as Gen 0 all early flashlights and "electric torches" that predate first-generation models defined next. Although Gen 0 includes a wide variety of devices, all are now out of production and obsolete, and hence of only historical significance.

Gen I lights comprise all flashlights that take modern alkaline batteries (e.g., cells in AA, C, and D sizes), including those cheap plastic or metal consumer models not specifically intended for law-enforcement or tactical use. Consumer flashlights are best suited for light-duty household applications. While they will serve in a pinch for defensive or tactical use, you're well advised to select a more task-spe-

48

First and second generation flashlights. From left: Gen I EverReady and Ray-O-Vac household models, 3 D-cell Streamlight, 5 D-Cell Mag Light, Mini-Mag, Tac Star T45, Mag Light Mag Charger, Streamlight SL-20. (Clay Babcock)

cific example for serious purposes. The angle head plastic GI flashlight is also of this basic design.

Of more interest here are Gen I law enforcement lights, the brainchild of California inventor Don Keller. In 1968 he introduced the Kel-Light, an aluminum bodied, alkaline battery design intended to provide police officers with a source of illumination that could double as a makeshift impact weapon in an emergency. It was an instant hit with the boys in blue.

If imitation is the sincerest form of flattery, then the Kel-Light has been extremely popular: a large number of near clones have sold well for many years. The Mag Light line produced by Tony Maglica's Ontario, CA, company is probably the most prolific example of a Gen I light, with other makers including Streamlight, Brinkman, and Bianchi jumping on the bandwagon. Both metal and polymer models are available.

Alkaline-powered penlights such as the Brinkman

Legend, Tac Star T-45, and the Mag Light Mini-Mag and Solitaire are also Gen I technology. However, light output with this type of implement is entirely inadequate for self-defense purposes. Even the big Gen I lights can be marginal in this respect. The search for the brightest possible beam resulted in the next stage of flashlight evolution.

In the early 1970s, Streamlight's full-sized, high-intensity rechargeables—such as their flagship SL-20 model—signaled the arrival of Gen II flashlights. Although outwardly resembling typical Gen I law enforcement designs, the second generation flashlights' light output is far greater than that of their predecessors due to advances in battery technology. They are economical to operate due to their nickel-cadmium (Ni-Cd) cells. The Mag Charger is another example of a Gen II light.

The third generation of flashlights is not one type, but a family of lights characterized by both small size and high light output. Gen III flashlights were pioneered by Laser Products president Dr. John Matthews with his weapon-mounted Sure-Fire lights. Initially developed to fill the needs of LAPD SWAT around the time of the 1984 Olympics, these early lithium battery-powered gun lights led directly to the hand-held Sure-Fire 6P, first sold during the late 1980s. The 6P set a new standard in terms of size, power, and beam quality.

Today, different configurations of Gen III lights are available for different tasks, and they fall into three basic categories. Hand-held models account for the first two Gen III categories: lithium-powered flashlights and rechargeable working flashlights. Which is best will depend on the application in question. Each offers relative advantages and disadvantages, which are largely a function of battery type, discussed in depth in a separate section below. The weapon-mounted lights used by most modern tactical teams and hostage rescue personnel are the third type of Gen III lights.

Lithium-powered flashlights are the smallest hand-held Gen III offerings. The classic Laser Products P series and their Sure-Fire CombatLights typify the breed; the Streamlight Scorpion, TACM III (hand-held), and ASP Tac

Third generation lights. Upper half of photo, clockwise from pistol: 6-volt Sure-Fire Tactical Light on Glock 17, Sure-Fire 12-ZM CombatLight, Streamlight Stinger, Sure-Fire 8X with leather holster, Sure-Fire 9N with Beamshaper holographic diffuser, Sure-Fire 9NT Turbo Head. Lower half of photo, counterclockwise from light on far right: Sure-Fire 3DL (infrared), Sure-Fire 6Z CombatLight in V-70 holster, Sure-Fire 9Z CombatLight, colored filters for Sure-Fire CombatLights, Streamlight Scorpion, Sure-Fire 6P (Clay Babcock)

51

Light are also in this category. Third generation rechargeables are far smaller than Gen II examples—a result of new compact Ni-Cd and nickel metal hydride (Ni-MH) batteries—and not much bigger than their lithium-powered relatives. Common examples include the Laser Products Sure-Fire models 8X, 9N, and Millennium PowerMax, and the Streamlight Stinger and Super Stinger.

This is probably as good a place as any to mention infrared flashlights. Employing an IR diode instead of a lamp filament to generate the beam, these devices provide greatly increased run time over a standard flashlight with IR filter and have greater (IR) light output as well. Obviously, to see such a beam requires some sort of NVE, and the primary tactical application for an IR light is in environments where there is inadequate ambient IR illumination, for instance indoors. In this application, I like to mount a Laser Products 3DL infrared flashlight pointing straight up on my helmet or weapon, bouncing the IR illumination off the ceiling while screening the red glow of the diode from view.

WEAPON-MOUNTED LIGHTS

Weapon mounted lights facilitate fighting with firearms in conditions of reduced illumination to a degree that often exceeds what is possible with NVE. With the beam boresighted to the gun, standard daytime firing techniques can be used. With proper switching hardware, the operator can use one hand to perform tasks such as operating a radio or opening a door while simultaneously supplying light and remaining ready to shoot.

A weapon mount is virtually the only feasible option for employing a light with a shoulder weapon (rifle, shotgun, submachine gun). Autopistols and revolvers are often used in conjunction with a hand-held light, but a weapon-mounted light is still by far the optimal solution. The alternative, using a hand-held light in conjunction with an appropriate flash-

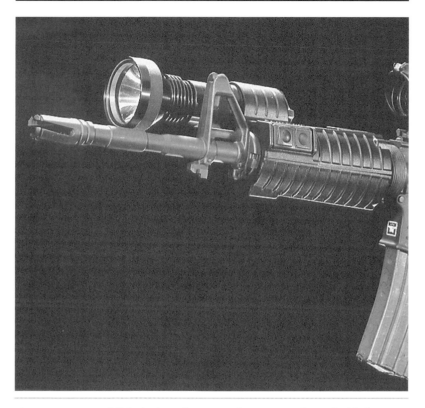

A weapon-mounted light is the only practical way to employ a flashlight in conjunction with a shoulder weapon. (Laser Products)

light-assisted handgun technique (e.g., Ayoob, Harries, Rogers/Sure-Fire, etc., described in Chapter 6) is certainly workable with adequate training, but clearly second best.

Exactly how the light is mounted to the weapon will vary with manufacturer and model. The best systems consist of a lamp module in a dedicated housing specific to the firearm in question, such as the Sure-Fire shotgun, MP-5, and M-4 mounts that replace the stock fore-end. This type of mount maximizes both ruggedness and ergonomics. A solid "universal" mount can be okay too, provided it is sufficiently sturdy and includes switching hardware that allows tactically correct operation. For sniper rifle applications Sure-Fire's weapon-mounted L120M "Leopard Light" provides the magnum illumination capability described below.

Lately, several companies have produced quick-detach hardware for securing a light to a firearm. Units by Diamond Industries, REF Instruments, and Glock mount the light to the bottom of a pistol magazine, which allows the handgun to be carried in most standard holsters with the light in place. The Heckler & Koch (H&K) Universal Self-loading Pistol (USP) features integral rails on the USP's frame to facilitate attaching a device such as their Universal Tactical Light. The latest Glocks, the Walther P99, and the SIGARMS sig pro include similar rails. A number of manufacturers make lights and lasers for these guns, including Laser Products (Sure-Fire), Insight Technologies, Wilcox, and Laser Devices.

Sage International makes a model that snaps onto the bayonet lug of an M-16 style rifle. And the Insight Technologies "Visible Light Module" uses Weaver-type clamps that affix a 9-volt lithium powered light to the Picattinny rail on the Knights Armaments Corporation Rail Interface System (described in the next chapter) on USSOCOM M-4 5.56 carbines.

The advantages of quick-detach models include the ability to reduce the physical envelope and weight of the weapon while the light is dismounted. Also, gun lights can be issued as required without special tools or weapon modification. On the downside, the user must predict the need for illumination in advance, and take time to affix the light. And with magazine mounts, you only have a light until you reload, unless all of your mags are similarly modified. If you use any type of detachable light, I recommend carrying the weapon with the device in place whenever possible unless sufficient ambient illumination is absolutely guaranteed, such as in daytime use outdoors. You'll also want to thoroughly test any gun equipped with such add-ons to ensure that weapon functioning is not affected.

Finally, some companies sell devices for fastening a hand-held light to your gun, using approaches from hose clamps to Velcro to gun-specific contoured mounts. The best of this breed is probably the old BEAMCO mount for the MP-5, which secures a full-sized Streamlight SL-20 to an H&K submachine gun. However, any time you strap a large flashlight to a gun, the bulk and weight of the light will negatively impact weapon handling characteristics. This is one reason small Gen III lights represent such an advance in the state of the art.

FLASHLIGHT FEATURES

A suitable momentary switch is probably the most important feature on a flashlight for gunfighting. Low-light tactics often dictate that the shooter use the light only when necessary and then only briefly; after extinguishing the light, he or she should generally move immediately relative to the most likely threat axis to prevent countertargeting. A switch without a true momentary capability is an invitation to disaster due to an unacceptable possibility of inadvertently turning the light on when you want it off. Fine motor coordination suffers greatly under stress, so forget about manipulating a click-on/click-off switch in a momentary fashion when your adrenaline is flowing.

On hand-held models the momentary switch should be located on the tailcap of the light, so it is orientation independent. (It is theoretically possible to build an orientation-independent side switch, but none are currently available.) There will not always be time to readjust the flashlight in the hand, and remember, we're talking here about working in the dark, so you'll have to operate largely by feel. The side switches on Mag Lights and the Streamlight Stinger are particularly tricky to find, being more or less flush with the body of the light. I know of one law enforcement user who painted a raised bead of nail polish on the body of his Stinger in line with the switch to facilitate finding it in the dark, but this is clearly a workaround.

A side switch also increases the risk of turning the light on while it is aimed backwards. Don't laugh; I've seen it happen.

With weapon-mounted lights the momentary switch(es) should be within reach when the shooter's hands are in a normal firing position. On shoulder weapons a trigger hand switch allows both weapon and illumination to be controlled with one hand while maintaining the ability to fire. However, using the support hand to control the light separates the functions of illumination control and weapon firing.

With a pump-action firearm, both the light and the switch(es) will need to be located on the fore-end. Note that coiled switch cords from a pump gun fore-end to a barrel- or magazine-tube-mounted light (e.g., Tac Star WLS-2000 or Lite Mount Technologies shotgun mounts) create an unacceptable risk of getting the cord snagged or caught in the action when it is cycled. In fact, all switch cords should be secured to the gun so they can't snag.

Constant-on capability is certainly required in many common circumstances, but the associated switching should ideally be physically separate from the momentary switch and/or require a dissimilar action to activate. Twist-on switches are a good way to accomplish this on a hand-held light and can be operated with one hand with a little practice.

With a weapon-mounted light, you'll want to have the ability to simultaneously supply illumination and shoot with one hand; this will require either a trigger-hand-activated momentary switch or a fore-end-mounted unit with both momentary and constant-on switching. A disable switch is also very useful, to prevent the light from inadvertently turning on, both in the carrying case and during an operation.

Lights that are attached directly to the firearm must withstand the forces generated when the gun discharges. The problem here is that lamp filaments are not particularly robust and are thus subject to breakage under the extreme acceleration of recoil, which is the greatest on handguns and shotguns. This is one drawback to simply bolting a standard hand-held flashlight to a handgun or shoulder weapon. The

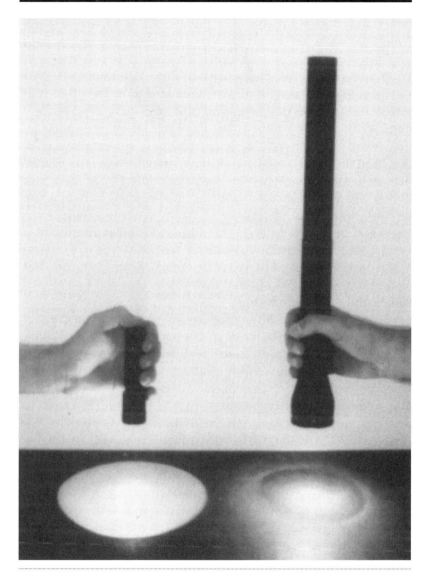

Compact third generation lights (Sure-Fire 6P, left) are capable of producing light output equal to the largest Gen I models (5 D-cell Mag Light), and slightly larger Gen III models can provide several times the output. (Laser Products)

lamp in a weapon-mounted light should be shock isolated from the body of the light. The best current approach to buffering the lamp is a compliant sleeve between the light body and lamp/reflector, as used in Sure-Fire lights.

In addition, Laser Products sells specially modified batteries for their classic weapon-mounted Sure-Fire tactical lights. The sets of two or three Duracell DL123A batteries—for 6-volt and 9-volt systems respectively—are encased together in a plastic sleeve. A fiber shock washer is placed between the cells to prevent battering due to recoil, and a nickel metal ribbon connector is spot-welded between the battery contacts to guarantee electrical continuity while firing. (The new Millennium series features a separate battery carrier that holds either three or six DL123A cells in a cloverleaf configuration.) All this may seem a bit extreme, but remember, we're talking about devices intended to be used in life-and-death situations.

As noted above, large size has historically been considered a positive attribute in a defensive/tactical flashlight. Certainly, a full-size aluminum flashlight provides significant perceived and actual potential as a makeshift impact weapon—contributing to officer "presence"—and can be held along the forearm for blocking. Plus a big light is easier to retrieve in the dark in the event that it is set down.

On the other hand, the advantages of small flashlights often outweigh the merits of long, heavy ones, provided light output is not unduly sacrificed. Bulk and weight of the device determine the possible on-body carry modes, i.e., type of holster, concealed or open wear, etc. Compact lights can also be held longer without user fatigue, and users with small hands will benefit greatly from a smaller-diameter light. Impact weapon defensive tactics are still possible using short-stick techniques (see Chapter 7). And as noted above, small size and light weight are important in a weapon-mounted light to minimize the impact on the firearm's handling characteristics.

BEAMS

The beam of a flashlight is its raison d'etre, and hence a good place to start when comparison shopping. Every beam consists of a bright central spot of reflected light surrounded by a less intense circle of illumination coming directly off the filament. The flashlight projects an ever-expanding cone of light, as can be seen by shining it along a wall. The intensity of any light decreases with the square of the distance.

What makes a good beam? First consider light output. Many flashlight ads tout a company's wares as providing the highest available candlepower, but this really doesn't tell you much. In actuality, candlepower numbers only describe the brightest part of the beam (i.e., "peak beam candlepower"). Note that a high candlepower figure says nothing about the beam configuration or the overall amount of light produced. A better unit of measure for comparison purposes is lumens, a metric unit of total light output.

To understand the difference between candlepower and lumens, picture a fire hose with an adjustable nozzle. The total amount of water coming out of the hose is analogous to lumens, with a narrow stream of water representing a higher peak candlepower figure than the same flow in a spray configuration. Just as the water pattern can be manipulated by turning the nozzle, peak beam candlepower can be increased or decreased by changing the reflector geometry. In any case, many published candlepower figures greatly exceed actual measured values.

For our purposes here, we can consider as "high intensity" any light with an output of more than 50 lumens. The beam from a five D-cell Mag Light with fresh batteries is about 65 lumens, as is that from a Sure-Fire 6P. Most Gen II and III rechargeables produce over 100 lumens of light. Bear in mind that eye response is logarithmic, not linear. Hence, you may not be able to perceive relative differences in power when near to the light source for lights with approximately the same output.

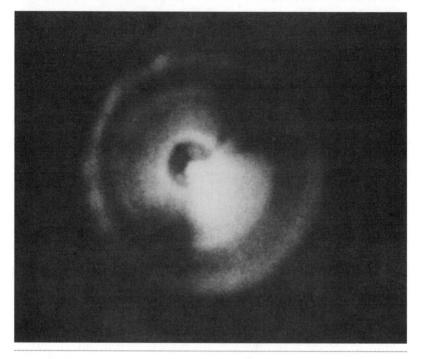

A focusable "spot-to-flood" reflector will never be perfectly in focus, resulting in dark spots, rings, and other irregularities. (Laser Products)

The latest breakthrough in flashlight power are the Sure-Fire Magnum lights (also known as blinding or dazzle lights) recently introduced by Laser Products. With an output of around 500 lumens—focused into a fairly tight beam—these devices (e.g., model 12P/ZM) provide an unprecedented ability to visually disable an adversary. Indeed, they raise the concept of light as a weapon to an entirely new level.

Other factors to consider with regard to the beam are quality and configuration. Ideally, the beam should be smooth and even, with no rings or dark spots. Achieving this goal requires the filament in the lamp to be located precisely at the focal point of the reflector, in three-dimensional space. So-called "focusable" flashlights merely move the lamp backward and forward and don't allow for sideways

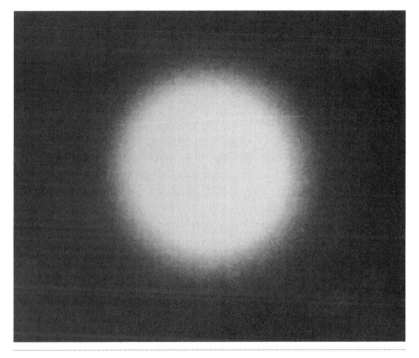

This perfectly smooth beam is the result of a factory precision focused lamp/reflector assembly. (Laser Products)

focusing. Hence they will inevitably provide a poor focus at even their best ("spot") setting.

Equally important, these "spot-to-flood" designs are apt to be significantly out of focus when you need them most, decreasing their illumination and blinding potential. If you must use a focusable flashlight, I recommend that you adjust it to its best (i.e., tightest, cleanest) setting, then tape, glue, or Loc-Tite it in place. In reality, adjustable beam flashlights are simply a way for manufacturers to use inexpensive flanged or bi-pin lamps and avoid the cost of accurately controlling the filament position. A far superior approach—though a bit more expensive to fabricate—is a precision prefocused lamp/reflector assembly, which will produce an optimum beam free from irregularities.

61

In general, the beam from a flashlight should be neither too narrow nor too wide; a compromise approach will illuminate the area of interest while allowing maximum situational awareness on the periphery. Currently, the Sure-Fire line from Laser Products sets the standard for beam quality. Not only is the lamp precision focused at the factory, but the reflector is textured with a proprietary surface to further smooth the beam.

Sometimes a tightly focused beam will be desirable, for instance when long-range illumination is required in rural environments, to look in to a "dark hole" (indoors or outside), or for maximum blinding effect. This is the purpose of the Gen III extended range flashlight, which can reach out to more than 100 meters in a hand-held configuration. The large reflector configurations on Laser Products' Sure-Fire lights—both lithium-powered and rechargeable models—comprises the only current examples of such flashlights.

The size of the reflector also contributes to the ability of a flashlight to visually disable an opponent. The larger the reflector, the greater the area on the subject's retina covered by the spot when the beam is viewed from the front. Coupled with an increase in the amount of light entering the eye, the bottom line is that for a given light output, the bigger the reflector, the more "blinding power" it has.

At the opposite end of the spectrum, you may want a broader, less intense beam for certain applications, for instance reading or writing. Once again, you want to achieve this characteristic without sacrificing smoothness. The "flood" setting on a focusable reflector is really just a severely out-of-focus beam. The best way to widen the existing beam without introducing irregularities is via a holographic diffuser, e.g., Sure-Fire Beamshaper. Mounted in a "pop-open" cover that slips over the head of the flashlight, a Beamshaper allows the user to choose instantly between a wide or general-purpose beam.

LAMPS

Lamp ("bulb") terminology can also be a bit confusing, so a brief primer on this subject is in order. The lamp is comprised of a wire filament inside a glass envelope, plus some type of electrical contacts to interface with the batteries. When sufficient current passes through the filament, it heats up and glows, providing light that can be focused by the reflector as described previously.

The exact size and configuration of the filament will depend on the system characteristics (i.e., voltage, current, etc.), and is really only of concern to the engineers who design such things. All you need to know is that it is important to use the correct lamp for the flashlight in question. For example, although it is possible to put a 9-volt lamp in a 6-volt system, light output will suffer dramatically. Conversely, the filament in a 6-volt lamp probably won't withstand the increased electron flow of a 9-volt flashlight, burning out instantly when the switch is turned on.

If the filament were exposed to the air, it would burn up at once. Hence, all oxygen must be removed from the glass envelope by way of a vacuum pump. Even then, when the filament heats up and glows, tungsten atoms are boiled from its surface. This does not occur in a uniform manner, and the resulting weak spot is what usually causes the lamp to ultimately fail.

Some of these tungsten atoms impact and coat the inside of the glass envelope, blackening it over time. If the lamp is filled with a noble (inert) gas, the molecules of the gas will deflect many of the tungsten atoms, preventing them from reaching the glass envelope. (Common household light bulbs contain the filament in a simple vacuum, but the glass envelope is many orders of magnitude larger than that of a flashlight. Hence, it doesn't blacken unacceptably during its useful life.) Cheap flashlight lamps use nitrogen instead of a noble gas.

The gasses most commonly used inside flashlight lamps are—in increasing order of density—argon, krypton, and xenon. The specific amount of gas inside the glass envelope will vary with manufacturer, with higher pressure equaling more gas equaling more expense. There is currently no standard as to the percentage of total gas that must be present to claim that the lamp is gas-filled. As with candlepower numbers, it's a situation of buyer beware, and once again a good rule of thumb is "you get what you pay for."

"Halogen" is yet one more term you will run into with respect to lamps, perhaps combined with one of the gases listed in the previous paragraph (e.g., a "krypton halogen lamp"). The halogen cycle is a process whereby tungsten atoms are removed from the glass envelope and redeposited on the filament. This becomes desirable once the power of the lamp exceeds a certain threshold.

With a high-intensity lamp, the heat generated is sufficient to melt a lexan lens if the light is left on for an extended period. For this reason, you should take care that your flashlight cannot be switched on inadvertently in carry or storage situations, for instance, by removing the batteries. Also, if oils from your fingers get on the glass envelope of a high-powered lamp, heat will often crack it. This is another strong point of the precision-focused lamp/reflector assembly: the unit can be handled by the outside of the reflector without touching the lamp at all.

BATTERIES AND CHARGERS

Battery type is another key parameter to consider when selecting a flashlight. Both Gen II and III designs, either Ni-Cd or lithium-powered, provide higher light output than alkaline battery-powered Gen I models for a given size. For example, a typical 6-volt third-generation lithium-powered light has a light output of 65 lumens—the same as a five D-cell first-generation alkaline flashlight—yet is just 10 percent as heavy and only 30 percent as long. And the latest compact Gen III rechargeables offer light output comparable to full-sized Gen II models; more in magnum versions.

Batteries and chargers. Clockwise from 9 o'clock: alkaline AA and D cells, Streamlight SL-20 trickle charger with Ni-Cd batteries for SL-20 (L) and Mag Light Mag Charger, Streamlight trickle charger and Ni-Cd battery for Stinger, Laser Products Rapid "Smart Charger" and Ni-Cd B92 battery for Sure-Fire 8X and 9N, lithium DL-123A batteries and Sure-Fire 6-volt tactical light cells. (Clay Babcock)

65

The primary advantages to alkaline batteries are run time and initial purchase cost. A fresh set of alkaline cells will provide several hours of light, albeit at a steadily decreasing output, for a couple of bucks. Common sizes of alkaline cells are the cheapest batteries to buy, though Ni-Cd rechargeables are more economical over the long run. Besides being able to deliver only relatively low power due to high internal resistance, alkaline battery negatives include poor cold weather performance and a cardboard casing that will often leak electrolyte, ruining the flashlight.

The Ni-Cd batteries used in Gen II and Gen III rechargeables enable one to make a far more powerful light than with alkaline batteries. Total run times of around an hour are typical. Lately, "extended run" models have hit the market (e.g., Super Stinger) which double the run time, but with the trade-off of a light that is approximately twice as long and heavy.

The main disadvantage with Ni-Cd cells is that they self-discharge over time. Leave the light in a drawer for several months and the batteries will be nearly dead. Heat accelerates this process, so carrying the flashlight in a hot car increases the probability that the batteries won't last for the duration of a critical incident.

Lithium batteries, on the other hand, have a long shelf life—10 years or more. They are the most powerful for their size and hence are used in the smallest available high-intensity lights, but they are also more expensive to use than either Ni-Cd or alkaline batteries (around $5 apiece retail as of this writing). Hence, lithium batteries are usually not the best choice for constant use in low-risk situations, due to cost. They do, however, provide the best cold-weather performance. Once again, typical run time is around an hour, with light output decreasing relatively steadily over time.

In contrast with lithium batteries, one other inherent characteristic of Ni-Cd cells is that they give only a minute or so of warning before they run out of juice. This argues for having two lights—one Ni-Cd rechargeable, one lithium-powered—if you use a light constantly yet depend on having illumination in a life-and-death situation. The second light can also be used if the first one breaks, or as a loaner. Cops have been carrying backup guns for analogous reasons for years. The small size of Gen III lithium lights makes this an eminently feasible practice, one I strongly recommend.

By the way, there is no "memory" effect with modern rechargeable batteries. I suspect that loss of run time attributed to this nonexistent phenomenon may be attributable to measures taken to prevent it. Many flashlight users have been fully discharging Ni-Cd cells before recharging them, in a misguided attempt to preserve battery life. As a Streamlight technical flyer notes, this procedure will actually cause battery damage due to reverse charging. (See Appendix C for technical details.) For this reason, you should always turn off and recharge a rechargeable battery-powered light immediately after the light dims appreciably.

It goes without saying that if you use a rechargeable flashlight, you'll also need a charger. With all Gen II and some Gen III designs, the entire flashlight is placed in an overnight "trickle" charger to replenish the batteries. This can be a handy way to store a light, especially a full-size model, but it does prevent you from using the flashlight while it is charging. Also on the downside, this type of charger continues to supply a constant current to the batteries after they are completely recharged, damaging the cells over time due to the resulting heat. If the battery stick or light body is warm to the touch the cells are topped off, and you should remove the light/battery from the charger.

The latest technological advance in this area is the "smart" or "rapid" charger, which features a microchip that senses the slight voltage drop that occurs when the battery is fully charged. The circuitry then automatically reduces the current to a low maintenance level. This eliminates the potential for cell damage through "cooking" the battery. (The natural degradation of electrolyte occurs more quickly at higher temperatures, as do all chemical processes.)

Some chargers—both trickle and rapid type—charge the

batteries out of the flashlight, which facilitates keeping the light with you at all times. Gen III lights are small enough that they can be worn continuously in a belt holster, much like a handgun. Even if you don't wear a belt, a small lithium-powered flashlight can be carried unobtrusively in a pocket, pouch, or purse. For either type of light, consider carrying "reload" batteries. Since supplementary illumination can be as important to the outcome of a violent situation as a perse weapon, a fresh set of cells could be critical. You should also carry a spare lamp.

As this book goes to press, Laser Products has developed a couple of rechargeable lights that use nickel-metal hydride (Ni-MH) batteries, which have higher capacity than Ni-Cd cells. This advance manifests itself in longer run times and/or greater light output. Pros and cons vis-à-vis other battery types are similar to Ni-Cd cells (self-discharge, little warning of depletion, etc.).

RECOMMENDED FLASHLIGHTS

In selecting a light, you'll first need to decide on the type of device that is most appropriate for the job. Alkaline-powered models really do not provide sufficient light output for defensive or tactical applications. Hence, in my opinion, Gen I lights are only suited for administrative tasks, unless nothing else is available. Given the potentially deadly nature of the task at hand, it is foolish to use second-rate gear in defensive or tactical applications. Stick with Gen III flashlight technology unless there is an overriding reason not to do so (e.g., your agency mandates a particular light).

For use with a firearm, a dedicated weapon-mounted light is best, for the reasons discussed previously. Don't fall into the trap of assuming that this equipment is only for SWAT team members. On the contrary, a weapon-mounted light is ideal for the private citizen who doesn't practice as much as he or she should. Such individuals are unlikely to master a hand-held-light-assisted handgun technique to the point that it is reflexive under stress. Mounting the light directly to the gun—with a pressure switch that can be activated in a normal firing grip—represents a turnkey solution to tactical illumination.

Characterized by solid mounts, shock buffering of critical components, and a wide range of switching options, the Sure-Fire line from Laser Products is the hands-down choice of armed professionals worldwide. Most of my long guns and several of my pistols sport dedicated Sure-Fire mounts, with the latest Millennium systems being the preferred option when available for the gun in question.

Although the quick-detach H&K UTL is a neat concept—and the side-by-side battery position makes for a short overall length—the reflector is of the spot-to-flood variety. The Sure-Fire USP tac light is far better, due to superior shock isolation of the lamp, factory precision focused reflector, and the ambidextrous "Slimline" switch.

In many situations a hand-held light will be needed, e.g., while performing tasks during which you don't want to point a gun at everything you're illuminating. For heavy nighttime use, a rechargeable model is by far the most cost-effective option.

The Ni-Cd-powered Sure-Fire model 9N has all of the desired beam and switching characteristics and features a dual-lamp system that offers high- and low-beam settings in the same device. (The 140-lumen high-power lamp will run for 40 minutes, the 20-lumen low-power lamp for 2 hours). The Ni-Cd batteries can be replenished either in the light or out, depending on charger configuration.

If you're on a tight budget, the Sure-Fire 8X is a smaller, less expensive rechargeable that includes all key switching and beam requirements. This 110-lumen Ni-Cd-powered flashlight is not much larger than a 9-volt lithium light and rides unobtrusively in a belt holster. Batteries are charged out of the light and give about an hour of run time.

Lastly, the new Sure-Fire Millennium PowerMax Model M2000, which I have examined in prototype form, may well obsolete all of the rechargeable flashlights currently in use

The latest third-generation lights comprise the Sure-Fire Millennium series by Laser Products. The M500 Millennium WeaponLight replaces the issue hand-guards on an M-4/CAR-15 carbine, such as this example that also sports an ACOG optical sight and Smith Vortex flash suppressor. (Laser Products)

by law enforcement. It provides both operation and magnum light from the same flashlight. The flashlight's patented switch system, located on the back end of the flashlight body, allows the user to select between the two beams the flashlight produces by simply varying the amount of pressure applied to the switch.

Press gently and you get 110 lumens of perfectly focused "operational" light. Press harder and the PowerMax M2000 emits 500 lumens of "magnum" light in a beam optimized in shape and intensity for temporarily blinding suspects. Switching back and forth between beams is essentially instantaneous. Should the user be confronted with a threat, the switch to the blinding beam will occur almost automatically due to a tightened grip on the flashlight. The M2000 uses Ni-MH batteries, and its run time is more than twice as long as older rechargeables (over two hours.)

A lithium-powered version (M2100) is also in the works, as is a Ni-MH rechargeable model with a single reflector head that produces operational light only (M1000). Both rechargeable PowerMax models employ the same advanced smart charger, which charges the Ni-MH batteries in the flashlight, and which twist locks into the charger (a safety feature when the charger is mounted inside a vehicle). The PowerMax lights are slated to hit the streets about the same time this book does.

A lithium-powered flashlight is the optimum choice for emergencies if you don't want to affix the light to your handgun but still want to use them together—for instance, when carrying concealed. To keep the batteries completely fresh, this "shooting light" should not be used for routine tasks. And, as noted above, if you really need a light, carry at least two. This SOP includes backing up weapon-mounted lights with hand-held models, both for illuminating things at which you don't want to point a gun, and in case the weapon-mounted light fails. The best alternative is a backup that uses the same lamp/reflector as the light on your gun(s) so you can cannibalize it if need be.

For a lithium-powered shooting or backup light, I like the Sure-Fire CombatLights—in particular the Millennium M1 model and the classic 9Z, which lend themselves to use as small impact weapons (details in Chapter 8). The smaller 6Z is another reasonable option for applications in which minimum size is desirable, e.g., concealed carry. CombatLights feature a contoured body with rubber grip rings to facilitate the Rogers/Sure-Fire shooting technique (described in Chapter 6) and work well with the the stalwart Harries technique too. All CombatLights come with a lanyard to prevent losing the flashlight when performing weapon manipulations such as clearing stoppages.

If you prefer a standard body configuration, the classic 6P and its bigger sibling the 9P give the same output as corresponding CombatLights (65 lumens and 105 lumens respectively). By the time you read this a 105 lumen lamp/reflector assembly for the 6-volt lights should be available, with a run time of approximately 20 minutes. The one-cell, 15 lumen 3P is not really powerful enough for tactical use but is a great utility light. All lithium-powered P and Z series Sure-Fire lights have a nominal one-hour run time.

The newest lithium-powered magnum light from Sure-Fire is the Millennium M2. It provides the same beam intensity as the 12ZM and 12PM hand-held lights. The M2 can run longer and continuously, and it uses six batteries arranged in a cloverleaf configuration to reduce overall length. The blinding power of these focused 500-lumen lights is truly awesome, on par with some of the spotlights described below at close range. They can serve as formidable nonlethal options, and I personally know of one case in which use of a 12ZM caused a perpetrator to drop a large knife during a dynamic SWAT entry.

Laser Products also makes a couple of convertible lithium/Ni-Cd Sure-Fire lights, the model 7Z CombatLight and the model 6R. The former accomplishes the conversion via a cylindrical spacer used with lithium batteries, and the latter is shortened by removing the center section of the flashlight body. Light output is 50 lumens—the lamp is optimized for long life instead of maximum power—and run time is 35 minutes with Ni-Cd batteries, one hour with lithium cells. I feel these models are best suited to low-risk situations or training, with a set of lithium batteries held in reserve for emergencies such as natural disasters.

Certainly all lights should be as water-resistant as possible. O-ring sealing and rubber switch gaskets are a must. If you need true underwater performance, however, you'll have to purchase a purpose-built light. Laser Products has provided such specialized hardware to maritime units like the U.S. Navy SEALs for years.

When you need illumination in an environment with flammable and/or explosive fumes, a nonincindive flashlight will be required. The UL and OSHA certification which is required of these lights takes into account such factors as whether the batteries can be inserted backwards and the ability of a spark from the circuitry to ignite vapors outside the light in the event the light is crushed. Pelican Products, perhaps best known for their molded hard plastic carrying cases, also makes a line of flashlights that includes nonincindive models with a class 1, division 1 rating—the highest available. Note, however, that these are all relatively low-powered lights, and the switching leaves much to be desired.

If you want a full-size high-intensity flashlight, the aluminum Streamlight SL-20 and SL-35 are probably the best of the breed. On the plus side, they provide decent light output and feature a factory focused lamp and reflector. Unfortunately, the switch on each is of the click-on type, mounted on the side of the light near the head. Also, the only charger available for the big Streamlights is an overnight "trickle" device. None of this is surprising considering that these are Gen II lights.

Even Gen III Streamlights—i.e., Stinger and Scorpion—use click-on switches (side-mounted on all versions of the Stinger except the XT) and focusable reflectors. So do all current Mag Lights. As of this writing Mag Light does not offer a rapid charger. Additionally, the rubber sleeve on the Scorpion and Poly Stinger, and the foam handle on the polymer SL-20, tend to bind on flashlight holsters and can eventually shred or tear. Even though these lights are intended for the police market, they leave something to be desired in this application for the reasons noted above. Of course, that said, any powerful flashlight is better than none.

At this point you may be wondering why Laser Products' Sure-Fire line stands head and shoulders above the competition in the area of hand-held and weapon-mounted lights. The reason is simple: LP president, Dr. John Matthews (a Ph.D. electrical engineer) has had extensive firearms and tactical training and serves as a technical reserve with the special operations unit of a local police agency. The result is an above-average understanding of what is needed in an illumination tool for serious purposes—knowledge that is reflected in the designs of the flashlights made by his firm.

Whatever light you choose, augment it with accessories as appropriate for your particular application. Owners of Gen III flashlights can take advantage of the large selection of flashlight holsters currently available—both flapped designs of leather or nylon, plus leather and composite models with friction retention. Either type is a great improvement over the ring carriers used in the past, which were not particularly secure and allowed the light to bang against the owner's leg whenever he or she would run. For concealed carry with a small lithium light, the combination magazine/flashlight carriers from Mitch Rosen (leather), Blade Tech (Kydex), and others are hard to beat.

Speaking of holsters, if you have a handgun-mounted light, you'll want to procure a suitable holster to carry it. The best such scabbards are the model 3004 and 6004 by Safariland, plastic tactical "leg rigs," the latter of which features the new self-locking hood-retention system. The only downside is that the holster has an open muzzle, and hence will not mask a "white light" unintentional discharge in the holster. Other options include the excellent line of ballistic nylon holsters from Eagle Industries, similar gear from Blackhawk, and nylon duty and tactical rigs by Michaels of Oregon.

Filters can modify the color of the beam for a specific purpose. The most common such are red (minimal impact on dark adaption), blue (highlights blood and is less visible to some Gen II and III NVE), amber (to best penetrate fog and smoke), and infrared (for augmenting ambient IR illumination when using NVE). If the filter is mounted in a pop-open lens cover, the user can convert instantly to white light.

For hands-free operation, a number of companies sell a variety of nylon and elastic headbands and wristbands to secure a small light directly to your body. A removable star-shaped rubber sleeve for the head of the light, sold as the "flashlight chock," will keep the light from rolling away when you set it down. And one final esoteric flashlight accoutrement—which provides increased safety for the patrol officer—is the snap-on colored translucent plastic cone that mounts over the head of the light to enable it to serve as a wand for directing traffic at night.

Flashlights and related accessories will continue to evolve as the result of technological breakthroughs. The inevitable result will be devices that are both brighter and smaller. As we go to press, Sure-Fire is introducing its new Millennium series of lights, mentioned above; I can vouch for the increase in capability they provide. Using the above discussion as a starting point, you should be able to evaluate the merits of any further developments with respect to your specific tactical applications.

SPOTLIGHTS

When the situation requires more illumination than is available in a hand-held or firearm-mounted light—and size and weight are not an issue—some type of spotlight may be the answer. Tools in this class typically provide much greater light output than even the brightest flashlight, and hence are capable of projecting a beam much farther than their smaller cousins. Blinding Power is also greater due to reflector size.

Prior to the widespread issue of NVE, searchlights played a key role in nighttime military operations. Readers are undoubtedly aware of the use of large searchlights in the antiaircraft role in World War II, and such equipment has been used in ground combat as well. (For a reasonably accurate depiction of powerful lights in action during the Korean War, watch the movie *Pork Chop Hill* starring Gregory Peck.) When image intensification gear is available, a large IR or visible searchlight bounced off cloud cover can provide a significant increase in light on the scene; this type of bistatic employment was used frequently in the Vietnam war under the code name Cyclops.

Today, use of visible spotlights by U.S. armed forces is generally limited to defensive operations, since the beam betrays the presence of the troops using the device. One exception is certain interdiction or roadblock missions during low-intensity conflicts, where the potential enemy is decisively outnumbered. Still, the use of visible light in offensive combat by today's troops is the exception rather than the rule.

In contrast with such specialized use by the military, spotlights are a staple source of illumination for the law-enforcement community. The most common police applications for large lights are various vehicle-mounted versions.

Patrol cars commonly supplement their headlamps with one or more aimable spotlights, plus fixed high-intensity lamps mounted to the emergency light bar—both forward-facing "take down lights" and side-mounted alley lights to facilitate viewing to the oblique. Likewise, the circling police helicopter piercing the darkness with a powerful beam is a familiar sight in large cities. And harbor patrol officers, too, depend on large spotlights for nighttime visibility.

If you don't want to permanently alter your vehicle to look like Car 51 or Adam 12, I suggest the GoLight detach-

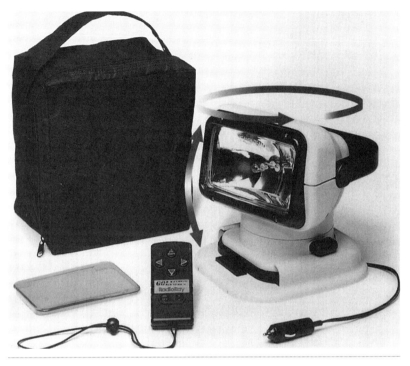

The GoLight RadioRay remote-controlled vehicle spotlight mounts in seconds using a suction base. (GoLight)

able spotlight. This high-powered unit includes a detachable suction base, plus a power cord that plugs into the cigarette lighter and features an in-line remote control with an on/off switch plus buttons for steering the beam. For a bit more money, you can buy the "RadioRay" version, which uses a wireless remote. Less expensive consumer-grade vehicle spotlights are available at any discount department store.

Bicycle officers and others who ride at night will also require some sort of vehicle illumination. The Night Sun system used by many departments consists of dual forward-facing high-intensity lamps mounted to the handlebars, powered by a battery configured like a standard water bottle and carried in the bottle rack on the frame. Nite Rider offers a similar system. Helmet-mounted lights (e.g., Night Sun "Sun Sport") are another viable alternative for the bike officer, or even the tactical operator who wants both hands free.

Portable hand-held spotlights can also have utility for use by tactical teams and high-risk warrant service personnel. Typical examples achieve requisite battery capacity with a carrying case or a harness to tote multiple cells connected in series. Some ballistic shields mount a small spotlight or Gen III flashlight. Though a bit large for all-day carry, this type of device can be valuable on raids and SWAT operations, for either interior or perimeter applications. I have personally used a hand-held version as a dedicated "light man" during force-on-force CQB training—a Maxa Beam MBS-410 with battery belt and push-button "spot-to-flood" capability—and can attest to its value.

Incidentally, a "focusable" beam isn't quite so bad indoors once there is sufficient light output (which is to say far more than what's available in even a Gen III hand-held flashlight). On a large spotlight, the tightest possible "spot" setting is good for looking into dark holes at quite some distance. And even though the "flood" setting is out of focus, light reflecting off the walls and ceiling fills in the gaps and covers large areas better than the tight beam can.

During a low-light seminar I gave at the 1997 International Use of Force Conference on Long Island, an NYPD cop showed me a home grown portable spotlight cobbled together from a "50,000 candlepower" Coleman replacement lamp, a couple of Gates rechargeable batteries, and a sturdy metal card file to hold the cells. Not surprisingly, it featured both momentary and constant on switches. The patrolman who made it said that whenever he used this device in support of Emergency Services Unit (i.e., SWAT) personnel, the ESU cops inevitably tried to walk off with it.

On the downside, the size and weight of large spotlights will always be a limiting factor with regard to their use in the manportable role. Even so, I predict that as the advantages of tactical illumination become more widely understood, portable spotlights will evolve into even more useful implements. My educated guess is that these devices will become both smaller and more powerful and include such features as wireless remote switching and beam steering.

Corrections officers are another class of law enforcement personnel that can benefit from spotlights. Whether from fixed perimeter lighting or a flexible searchlight in a guard tower or gun truck, a high intensity beam is a key weapon for preventing, detecting, and defeating escape attempts, yard fights, and riots. Couple this with the fact that a hand-held flashlight may be the only "weapon" allowed prison guards, and it becomes clear that illumination tools are extremely important in this high-risk profession.

Home security is yet one more application in which a large light provides clear benefits. Criminals like to operate undetected. If an outdoor light turns on when a building is approached, the first thought most people have is usually, "I've been seen." The deterrent effect of this phenomenon should not be underestimated. Hence, every residence should have 360 degree coverage by motion detector floodlights, available at any discount department store.

Whether large or small, a self-supplied light will roll back the darkness to a degree undreamed of by our ancestors. When you consider that a majority of violent civilian confrontations occur in low light, it becomes clear that illumination tools are mission-essential equipment for defensive and tactical applications. This is particularly true in scenarios involving the use of deadly force. If the first rule of gunfighting is "have a gun," the second is probably "have a light."

chapter

5

ADDITIONAL TOOLS

ANY NUMBER OF ITEMS CAN contribute to success-
ful night fighting. Even if a particular piece of equipment
isn't specifically intended to serve as low-light gear, you'll
need to analyze how its design will affect your ability to successfully achieve your specific goals under conditions of
reduced illumination.

This chapter addresses a mixed bag of kit that can contribute to surviving a violent encounter in low light. It is not
intended to be all-inclusive, and your particular situation
may require additional hardware. As with the rest of this
book, the concepts discussed below are to be considered a
starting point.

CLOTHING

The stereotypical ninja assassin—clad in black from head
to toe—presents an image of a warrior prepared to infiltrate

81

in the darkness. For sure, what you wear can affect your ability to operate covertly. However, in most low-light environments the best color for clothing is not what you might think.

Whether indoors or out, there is usually some ambient light. Hence jet black attire is usually too dark, and frequently stands out against the background. Of course, you don't want something too far to the other end of the spectrum either. Many grays on the market are too light. And needless to say, bright, reflective, and shiny items should be muted or discarded. Some police supply catalogs sell dull grey badges for night shift use, or officers can wear a uniform top with an embroidered shield or star.

I have found that the best all-around color for low-light application is sage green, the color of Nomex flight coveralls. Night desert BDUs are also good: mottled green with a grid to confuse NVE, as are appropriate garments or load-bearing equipment rendered in olive drab or blue-gray (for instance, the O.D. tactical vest by Eagle Industries). You'll need to experiment to find what works best in your area of operations.

Since you often can't see the ground in front of you, a good set of boots with adequate support is a must to prevent injury. It's real easy to twist an ankle or blow out a knee at night. The rougher the terrain, the more sturdy your footwear will need to be. Additionally, the material and design of the sole can affect noise, particularly indoors; a number of makers sell boots expressly designed to reduce sound signature on floors.

Eye protection is also good insurance against injury. On the downside, goggles and glasses can reflect ambient light, plus have the potential to fog up. Your eyesight will be bad enough at night without the additional burden of opaque lenses. Hence, antireflection and antifog coatings should be used with all tactical eyewear. The latest Bollé goggles—designed to reduce the probability of fogging—are well-liked by SWAT and special operations personnel. Medical supply houses can provide you with "FRED," an antifog solution used by surgeons when working over steaming incisions.

Clothing for low-light operations includes sage green Nomex flight coveralls and night desert BDUs and smock. Also shown are Nomex gloves and balaclava, elbow and knee pads, and Night Sun head lamp. (J.C. Ponce)

Head gear, too, should receive proper attention. Balaclavas are a good way to mask the face without having to resort to cammo paint sticks. These should be supplemented with a rigid helmet when appropriate. For instance, Pro Tec style skateboarding helmets are used by the U.S. Navy SEALs to prevent them from banging their heads on low bulkhead passageways, overhead plumbing, and so on.

Likewise, gloves should always be worn in low-light operations, to both hide and protect the hands. More than one operator has shoved his fist through a window on an op. I recommend sage green Nomex flight gloves with leather palms, available at most military surplus stores. Slash- and puncture-resistant Kevlar gloves are good too, and knee and elbow pads aren't a bad idea either.

Lastly, the day is rapidly approaching when military personnel will need to wear clothing that hides their heat signatures—"thillie suits"—to defeat targeting by thermal weapon sights. A Mylar "space blanket" will accomplish the same thing. The Border Patrol has encountered illegal aliens wearing several trash bags to mask body heat from thermal imagers used by that federal agency. Keep in mind that any such garments bring with them a high risk of dehydration-induced casualties.

CHEMICAL LIGHT STICKS

Cyalume light sticks consist of a flexible, translucent, cylindrical plastic tube containing two chemicals that glow when mixed. They were developed at the Naval Weapons Center, China Lake, CA (where, coincidentally, I worked for 10 years as a Department of Defense military operations analyst). The original purpose for this technology was survival signaling by downed aircrews, with the military quickly discovering other applications.

In storage configuration, one of the liquids is separated from the other in a brittle plastic container inside the flexible outer envelope. To activate, flex the light stick to break the inner vial, then shake vigorously to mix. The stick will typically glow for several hours, with output decreasing gradually over this time.

Light sticks come in a variety of sizes and colors, including infrared versions. How they are employed is limited only by your imagination. The most common use for light sticks in a combat scenario is marking people, equipment, or routes. Sticks can be fastened to the backs of team members to keep track of progress and to prevent fratricide. Law-enforcement personnel can use them as landmarks, for instance, on the way to a raid location.

Light sticks can also be used for illumination, although output is pretty meager compared with most other tools. An acquaintance who does special operations consulting for the Jordanian government relates using IR chem lights to supplement ambient light during a night ambush conducted using NVE and mortars. To achieve a useful degree of illumination, he had to hang literally dozens of light sticks in a tree adjacent to the kill zone.

This is also a good place to mention road flares. While hardly a general purpose tool, they are widely available and generate more light than a cyalume stick. Parachute illumination flares are even better, but usually a military proposition. Unlike chem lights, a flare constitutes a fire hazard, and application is limited by this characteristic. Neither light source can be "turned off" easily, though the flare can be extinguished and a light stick buried or otherwise hidden from view, for instance in its wrapper.

PERIMETER DEFENSE

Most people sleep at night, so some passive means of maintaining security during this period is a must. This can either take the form of a physical impediment or some sort of alarm. Just realize that any barrier can be breached with enough time and effort and should hence be considered primarily as a delaying tactic. Likewise, the word "alarm" originally meant a call "to arms," so you'll need to have the capability to backup the call with active measures when necessary.

Fences and walls are a tried and true approach to an outer perimeter; note that you can see and shoot through the former, in either chain link, barbed wire, or electric versions. Razor ribbon is especially effective, either on its own or to top off a wall or fence. Thorny shrubs can augment any of these man-made obstacles. Clear a sufficient area inside and/or outside of the barrier(s) to permit observation of anyone trying to cross. (In military parlance this is the "kill zone.")

For building security, quality dead bolts are essential. An office or bedroom door lock will provide an additional layer of protection. Various and sundry ancillary locking devices—for example, the "Door Club"—can increase the time required to defeat the door. Ornamental iron burglar bars on windows will keep intruders out, but this must be weighed against the fact that they may prevent emergency egress in case of fire.

Different types of sensors can be integrated with a barrier or used as a stand-alone system. Technological advances in this area include infrared, seismic, and microwave detectors hooked up to floodlights and/or audible/visual signals. In a building or other structure, switch contacts connected for an alarm can be installed on doors and windows. Tried and true low-tech approaches such as the empty tin cans on concertina are still viable options. And, of course, military users can employ trip wires attached to either flares or mines, plus mine fields per se.

Which brings us to booby traps. Unless you are in a war zone, don't even think about it! The law expressly proscribes the use of any type mechanical device that operates autonomously as judge, jury, and executioner. The risk of jail term or lawsuit outweighs the benefits of potentially injurious and/or lethal man traps for civilian users.

DOGS

One of the best low-light fighting systems around has four legs and fur. The military has recognized this for years and has used working dogs in scout and tracking applications, plus situations involving land mines and tunnels. In general, a well-trained dog should primarily be considered a highly capable sensor, with only secondary employment in the attack role.

Dogs can hear frequencies both above and below the range of the human ear. They also have a phenomenal sense of smell, 4 to 7 million times more sensitive than that of a human. And while a dog's eyesight does not provide very good depth perception—being akin to rod vision in a human—it is far superior in low light to that of a person. The upshot of all this is that a dog can detect a person at up to several hundred meters at night if conditions are right.

As with human performance, the key to canine capability is training. This includes both the initial schooling of the

A well-trained dog may be the ultimate night-fighting sensor system. (Jane C. Kirkland)

87

animal (months, not weeks) plus enough additional time with the handler that the dog bonds with its master. The handler must be able to "read" the behavior of his or her animal instantly, especially at night. A good rule of thumb is that it takes at least one year of the handler and dog working together constantly before this process can be considered complete. For our purposes here, it is also important that sufficient time be spent training in the dark.

In nighttime work, the recommended means of tethering handler to dog is with a 30 foot "long line" made of tubular nylon webbing. Carry several of these so that the line can be cut should it become entangled. The handler can tell by the pull on the line if the dog is "on track." Other possible ancillary equipment includes IR diodes on the collar so that the dog can be instantly located using NVE. In fact, one law enforcement K-9 officer of who often operates with NVGs actually mounts a set of IR lights on his dog's harness to provide standoff IR illumination!

With regard to breeds, the German shepherd is the hands-down favorite, comprising 80 percent of the working dogs in the world. A popular saying with professional canine trainers is that "German shepherds don't do any one function the best; they do everything second best." Which makes them the best utility dog.

Other good breeds include the Beauceron—which is extremely agile and has great endurance—and the Malinois. Both resemble the shepherd somewhat. The U.S. Army has fielded black Labrador retrievers in the past, both due to coloration and high drive. The DOD estimates that 50,000 casualties were avoided during the Vietnam war through the use of dogs. (The U.S. military also employed explosive-laden "kamikaze collies" to take out bunkers during World War II, but I digress.)

Some breeds many people think of in the combat role are in reality not the best choices. Rottweilers can be stubborn and simply do not have the stamina for extended operations. Similarly, the Doberman pinscher is largely overrated, being hyperactive, not as intelligent as the shepherd family, and prone to health problems. A Dobie is best suited as a free-ranging protector of large fenced areas, as is a pit bull. Of course, a dog of any kind can serve as an early warning system. So can geese.

EDGED WEAPONS

I'm sure many readers carry a knife on a daily basis, either in the field or as insurance in the event of a lethal assault in an urban or suburban environment. The knife-bearing individual should welcome conditions of reduced illumination and be prepared to exploit the advantages thereof. With a little forethought, the odds can be further stacked in your favor through the selection of an appropriate knife suited to the fighting style in question—one with features optimized for low light.

Whether the blade is fixed or folding, its surface is the key low-light attribute. As attractive as a fine mirror polish can be, it has no place on a night-fighting tool. Reflections off your knife can betray your presence, give away your intentions prematurely, and make techniques easier to counter. A dull, bead-blasted finish is one way to subdue the shine. Some sort of coating on the blade (e.g., black titanium carbonitride, aka black ti) is another.

Arguably the favorite edged-weapon option these days—popularized by the Spyderco Clipit series—is a lock-blade folder with a pocket clip and some means to facilitate one-handed deployment (e.g., hole in the blade, opening stud, or disk). One can now choose from a plethora of production knives. The Spyderco Military comes in a black blade version, as do the popular Benchmade AFCK and offerings from makers such as Ernest Emerson and Allen Elishewitz. Automatic openers ("switchblades") such as those by Benchmade and Microtech are potentially noisy. (The latter company offers a unique "double-action" knife that will function in manual mode as well.)

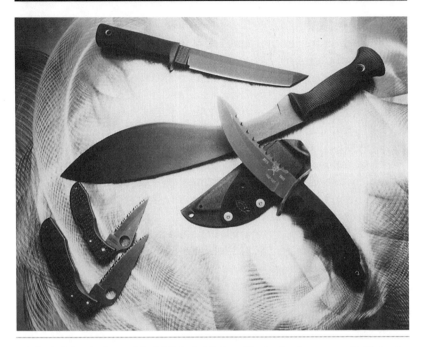

Night-fighting knives with dull black blades. Clockwise from top: Cold Steel Recon Tanto, Cold Steel LTC Kukri, Hobbit Warrior from Round Eye Knife and Tool, Spyderco Endura, Spyderco Delica. (Clay Babcock)

For those who want a fixed-blade knife, there are literally dozens of suitable models. Except where otherwise noted, all of those listed herein can be ordered with some type of black blade. For concealed carry, I highly recommend the MCS knives from Bud Neally (Pesh Kabz, Aikuchi, and Kinzal), the Jashido Compact by James S. Piorek, and the Hobbit's Fang from Round Eye Knife and tool. I also like Cold Steel's double-edged push daggers for defensive applications, but unfortunately the blades are somewhat shiny. Who knows? Maybe Cold Steel President Lynn Thompson will read this and come out with a dull black version.

For open carry, there is any number of larger general-purpose models that can double as a weapon should the need arise. The Buck Nighthawk, in black of course, is an economical choice of medium size, and the Cold Steel Recon Tanto is a good way to go if you like a chisel-point configuration. Plus, there are numerous custom designs.

If you prefer a chopping implement, the kukri makes an excellent low-light weapon. The Gurkha soldiers who carried them actually preferred night attacks. Anything that gets in the path of these Nepalese knives is likely to be cleaved or severed completely. Hence, targeting is not as critical as with a small blade, provided you follow up as required. Cold Steel's matte black LTC and Lightweight Gurkha kukris are well suited to low-light use. A large Bowie will also provide the ability to chop. Ontario knives in Franklinville, NY, makes a relatively inexpensive Bowie in black, as well as offering a variety of serviceable black swords.

Lastly, the specialized Warrior design by Bob Taylor and Randy Wanner is intended for reverse-grip use, which implies maintaining close contact with the enemy. With a good hilt to prevent the hand from slipping onto the blade when stabbing, large serrations on the back of the blade to facilitate hooking extremities (much like a preying mantis claw), and a hexagonal pommel for impact strikes with the butt of the knife, the Warrior offers a wide variety of ways to inflict damage. The Hobbit version by Round Eye Knife and Tool is currently the best of the breed.

With any fixed-blade knife the sheath must allow for the silent withdrawal of the blade. Here is one place where leather may actually have an advantage over Kydex, since the latter material can clatter as the knife is removed quickly. Some Kydex scabbards provide a means of disengaging the retention detent with the thumb, which can aid with noiseless presentation. Custom maker James Piorek combines the best of both worlds with his leather-covered Kydex sheaths. In any case, you should experiment until you find a technique that will let you draw your weapon without making a sound, then practice until it is reflexive.

FIREARMS AND ACCESSORIES

When selecting a primary weapon, most 20th century warriors opt for a gun. Presumably, this trend will continue into the next millennium. One private sector firearms training establishment notes in its motto, "Any gun will do, if YOU will do." True enough. Still, it helps to have the right tool for the job. In addition to the normal characteristics of a suitable fighting firearm—extreme reliability, good ergonomics, adequate practical accuracy—there are a couple of traits that are particularly relevant at night.

First of all, shooters must contend with firing signature (i.e., noise and muzzle flash), which can give away your location to an adversary, plus destroy your dark adaption and hearing. For these reasons, minimizing or eliminating visible and audible byproducts of weapon discharge is highly desirable.

The second attribute you'll want is sustained rapid-fire capability. This is a function of both the ammunition capacity of the weapon, plus recoil and muzzle rise characteristics of the cartridge it chambers. Please note, I am not advocating a "spray and pray" or "hose and hope" approach to low-light shooting problems. Rather, the need for follow-up shots is a natural consequence of the fact that you may miss more at night.

Concerning firing signature, there are a couple of ways to reduce the muzzle flash of a given cartridge. First is selection of weapons and ammunition. Be aware that shorter-than-average barrels tend to exhibit greater flash and blast. With regard to ammo, you'll need to experiment with a variety of loads to find out which, if any, minimizes the sound and fury. Some companies use low-flash powders wherever possible. (Also see the book *Handgun Muzzle Flash Tests*, available from Paladin Press.)

While on the topic of ammunition, I should mention tracers. While tracer rounds will certainly help you to walk your rounds onto the target in the dark, it usually takes several shots to achieve a hit. Hence, such ammunition is unsuitable for use in most civilian scenarios, whether by law enforcement or private citizens. Additionally, they constitute a fire hazard and are unlawful in many jurisdictions. On the other hand, military units can benefit from using tracers, particularly in belt-fed, crew-served weapons. Personnel equipped with night vision goggles or weapon sights can use tracers to direct the fire of team members without NVE. Just remember, tracers work both ways!

Back to muzzle flash, the other means of eliminating this signature is via a flash suppressor/hider, or a sound suppressor (silencer). The Smith Vortex flash suppressor—based on a WWII German design, with a literal twist so it could be patented—virtually eliminates flash even on short barrels. Unfortunately, the Clinton "Crime Bill" proscribes flash suppressors as evil, so you'll need to obtain a preban gun to remain within the law when installing one. Actual silencers

Sound suppressors ("silencers") have great utility at night, since they attenuate or eliminate muzzle flash as well as noise. Three "cans" from Knight's Armament Corporation, from top to bottom: M-4 5.56 carbine, SR-25 7.62 rifle, Mk23 Mod 0 SOCOM offensive handgun. (Doug Miyatake)

This suppressed M-4 carbine mounts an Aimpoint sight and sports Sure-Fire light and AN/PAQ-4 laser aimer on its KAC Rail Interface System fore-end. (Ichiro Nagata, PDC)

are tightly regulated, but if you are willing to jump through the hoops to buy one, it will get the job done! AWC, Gemtech, and Knights Armaments Corporation (KAC) all make top-notch "cans."

What specific types of firearms do I recommend for nighttime use? In reality, any reliable pistol or revolver of caliber 9mm or .38 special and above will suffice. Those who won't obtain professional instruction and practice at least once a month are well advised to stick with a revolver, probably in .38 Special. Stay away from magnums, as they tend to exhibit excessive muzzle flash and blast.

For people who will put in the time and effort in training, a quality semi-auto handgun has certain advantages, specifically increased ammunition capacity and hit probability. Most quality semiautomatics from the major manufacturers in calibers 9mm parabellum, .40 Smith and Wesson, or .45 ACP are suitable for serious use. Though I have frequently carried a Colt Commander .45 auto in the past, my current advice is to go with the Glock line, unless you prefer something else. (I'm wearing a Glock 19 9mm as I write this.)

A shotgun is often recommended for low light combat—due to the spread of its projectiles—and it's not a bad choice. However, many people mistakenly believe that the smooth-bore throws a wide, alley-clearing pattern right out of the muzzle. In reality, the typical spread of buckshot loads is 1 inch per yard from the muzzle or a bit less. In any case, you'll want to get all pellets on target for maximum terminal effect and minimum risk to bystanders downrange. Hence you'll still have to aim it, day or night.

The primary advantages of the shotgun are that it strikes a hard blow, is easy to hit with under stress relative to a handgun, and presents a reduced risk of overpenetration (with buckshot) and a decreased maximum range compared to a high-powered rifle. Short-barreled 12-gauge pump or semiauto models from Benelli, Beretta, Remington, Winchester, and Mossberg are all serviceable weapons.

Modern semi-automatic rifles derived from military designs are generally the first choice in this class of small arm, though any centerfire repeating rifle will do in a pinch. My personal favorite is the Colt AR-15/CAR-15 and its clones—civilian versions of the U.S. M-16/M-4. They are lightweight, feature good human engineering, and are easy to shoot well under stress. The 5.56x45 NATO cartridge (.223 Remington) is plenty powerful for antipersonnel use at common combat ranges, and recoil is negligible.

If you haven't guessed, I consider a light mount to be a vital piece of ancillary equipment for all of the above. (In case you need corroboration, combat shotgun guru Louis Awerbuck—one of my great teachers—considers a light mount the number one accessory for a defensive smooth-bore.) Tritium sights are okay, too, within the limitations previously discussed, as are NVE weapon sights, laser aimers, and optical sights. I highly recommend the Sure-Fire Millennium M500 and M510 WeaponLight for the M-16 and

M-4 respectively. Lastly, the KAC Rail Interface System is yet another option for mounting lights and other low light equipment on the current U.S. service rifle and its derivatives.

All of the devices discussed in preceding chapters can assist you in surviving a low-light confrontation. Still, any piece of hardware is just a tool in your tactical toolbox. The best equipment in the world won't do any good if the operator isn't up to the task at hand. Therefore, the rest of the book will address how to get the most out of your ultimate weapon, which is YOU.

chapter 6

TECHNIQUES WITH FLASHLIGHT AND FIREARM

MANY PEOPLE RELY ON AN autopistol or revolver for their primary defensive firearm. And as noted in Chapter 4, a flashlight provides outstanding general-purpose utility in low light at a moderate cost. Thus, it follows that employing these two pieces of defensive kit together often represents both the preferred course of action and also the most likely due to relative affordability.

There are several ways to shoot and provide illumination at the same time. While a dedicated light mount is the best option, the average citizen armed with a handgun will often be equipped with a hand-held flashlight. The majority of police personnel, too, use their duty sidearm with a departmental-issue hand-held light. Fortunately, the problem of employing the handgun and flashlight in concert has been studied over the years, resulting in the development of a number of viable solutions.

This chapter will examine the most common means of augmenting a handgun with a separate flashlight. Various ways of using the two together have been devised by private sector schools and trainers. Police and military organizations have also developed light-assisted shooting techniques. The grandfather of these was taught by the Federal Bureau of Investigation (FBI) at its Quantico, VA, academy (and is also described by Ed McGivern in his book *Fast and Fancy Revolver Shooting.*

THE FBI TECHNIQUE

With the old FBI method, the handgun is fired with the unsupported dominant hand (i.e., right hand for a right-handed person), and the flashlight is held in the nondominant hand (or vice versa if required by the tactical situation). The flashlight arm is fully extended to place the light as far as possible from the shooter's body—at shoulder level or a bit higher—and the pistol is fired dominant hand only. The beam can be oriented in the flashlight hand in either of the

The classic FBI flashlight technique. (Clay Babcock)

two possible ways, with the palm up or down as needed to aim the light forward with a given switch location.

The stated purpose of shooting this way is to confuse the assailant about the actual location of the shooter relative to the source of the light. This sounds good in theory, but in an indoor scenario, reflected illumination from walls often gives the shooter's position away despite efforts to conceal it. Obviously, with this type of one-handed method, the light can be positioned a number of places relative to your body.

A variation of the FBI technique is taught by former U.S. Navy SEAL Ken Good, director of the Sure-Fire Institute and co-founder of Combative Concepts, Inc., along with his partner, SEAL Dave Maynard. Instead of holding the light out to the side, it is placed alongside the shooter's head or neck and used to illuminate the sights and target. The primary reason SFI/CCI uses this method is to reduce the amount of the shooter's body exposed when "clearing" a corner.

Sure-Fire Institute Director Ken Good demonstrates the variation on the FBI technique he popularized. (Andy Stanford)

The FBI and SFI/CCI techniques certainly allow for accurate shooting in darkness. On the downside, both techniques require the shooter to fire one-handed, with an attendant loss in stability and recoil control. He or she must align the beam and the gun independent of one another, which can take time that the shooter just doesn't have. Lastly, the standard FBI method is not well suited to firing from cover, since the light is displaced significantly away from the shooter.

This is not to say that one should never shoot this way. There are times when holding the light away from the gun may be the best tactic. For instance, you can lead with the light (as a distraction) when entering a bathroom or other constrained space. Holding the light high while firing low is a workable solution for shooting around cover. And the SFI/CCI technique is a good transitional stance when assuming the Harries technique described below. Nonetheless, for general purpose use I suggest one of the more recently developed methods that place an emphasis on indexing the light directly to the weapon, with the goal of improved hit probability.

THE CHAPMAN/ROGERS TECHNIQUE

The lineage of this method is not entirely clear. Some sources attribute its development to Ray Chapman, the first world IPSC champion and Director of The Chapman Academy. Or the method may have been developed by former FBI agent Bill Rogers. Perhaps it was discovered independently by both men. No matter who gets the credit, it's a good technique for use with a side button flashlight.

To assume the technique, the light is first encircled with the thumb and forefinger of the nonshooting hand, with the head of the flashlight protruding from the thumb side of the hand. The flashlight hand middle-, ring-, and little fingers wrap as a unit around the firing hand on the front strap of the handgun. Depending on your stance, these three fingers may point horizontally, vertically, or somewhere in between

*The Chapman/Rogers technique is well suited to small side-switch lights like
the Streamlight Stinger shown here. (Clay Babcock)*

on a diagonal. Recoil control is poorest when the support hand fingers are placed underneath in a "cup and saucer" hold, since this does virtually nothing to manage muzzle flip.

What works best for me when using this technique is to let the thumb provide most of the gripping of the flashlight, and to work the switch with the index finger. The opposite approach may be better for you. Experiment with both. In any case, a proper Chapman/Rogers technique provides excellent stability when employing a side button flashlight with your handgun.

The question arises, "If I hold the light in front of me with my gun, won't my adversary shoot at the light and hit me?" It's a valid concern, but one rooted in a reactive mind-set. The majority of today's top tactical trainers stress a proactive approach, i.e., using the technique that allows you to shoot most effectively, on the argument that if your adversary has been taken out of the fight, you don't need to worry about return fire. Chapter 8 will discuss additional tactics that can largely eliminate the negative aspects of using a light.

LFI: LETHAL FORCE ILLUMINATION

As an expert in the legalities of deadly weapons, Lethal Force Institute Director Massad Ayoob knows the critical importance of identifying your target before firing. Having studied defensive shooting for more than three decades, he also understands the need to deliver accurate fire quickly at close range in dim light. Therefore, it is no surprise that Ayoob set his mind to the task of shooting under conditions of poor illumination. The flashlight technique he developed is very quick to assume and provides a means of repeatably aligning a sidearm and hand-held light.

With the Ayoob technique, the flashlight is held in the nonshooting hand with the beam extending from the thumb side of the hand. The pistol is extended in front of the body in a one-hand hold, and the shooter simply places the flashlight-hand thumb next to the shooting-hand thumb, assuming an isosceles-type stance.

Massad Ayoob, self-defense trainer and author, shown here with his primary home-defense handgun: Beretta M92 9mm with Sure-Fire mount, extended barrel, and 20-round magazine. (Clay Babcock)

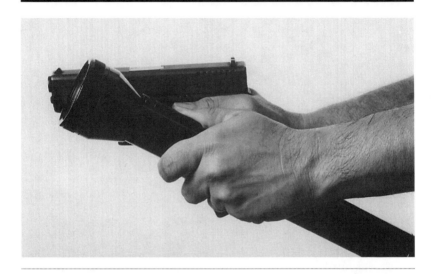

The original Ayoob technique places both thumbs parallel, resulting in the focused part of the beam passing over an adversary's head at much beyond contact distance. The Wenger variation places the flashlight-hand thumb underneath the gun-hand thumb, aligning the beam more closely with the weapon's bore. (Clay Babcock)

Author demonstrates the Wenger variation of the Ayoob technique using a Streamlight SL-20. (Clay Babcock)

105

With this thumb position, the beam points quite high in relation to the sights. Ayoob intended the light to shine in an assailant's eyes while pointing the handgun at the chest. In my experience, the focused part of the beam passes over the target at anything past arm's length. Former LFI instructor Steve Wenger modifies this technique slightly by rotating the light downward, positioning the flashlight-hand thumb lower than the gun-hand thumb; this aligns the beam of the light more precisely with the bore line.

Another spin on this type of quick, isosceles-style beam indexing was developed by USMC embassy guards. With a full-sized light, you can push the front of the light into the tips of the gun-hand fingers. Grip on the weapon is minimally affected, and some isometric tension can be generated to stabilize the pistol.

A similar effect can be achieved by setting the butt of the handgun on top of the flashlight. This is sometimes called the "over/under" or "New York" technique.

A flashlight with a side-mounted switch is required for the Ayoob, "over/under," and USMC techniques; lights with rear button switches cannot be used conveniently with this method unless they have been switched to stay on, often a tactical no-no. With a tailcap switch, you can hook the tips of the flashlight-hand fingers over the gun-hand thumb. This method is taught by Smith and Wesson Academy instructor Duane Deiter as part of his "power point" close-quarters combat system.

Each of these four techniques offers at best a tenuous interface between firearm and flashlight. Although they provide improved beam indexing compared with the FBI and SFI/CCI methods, there is really no positive interlock between the two hands for recoil control as there is with the Rogers/Chapman or the techniques described next.

THE HARRIES HOLD

In the early 1970s former Marine Michael Harries— regarded by Mas Ayoob as the most street-smart instructor to

Michael Harries demonstrates the handgun/flashlight technique named for him. (Clay Babcock)

Drawing safely into the Harries technique requires a process that extends the handgun first, then passes the light underneath: 1) Index the light to the centerline of the body; 2) move the light to the flashlight-side shoulder, as in the SFI/CCI technique, and draw the handgun to a close-quarters retention position; 3) extend the handgun into the SFI/CCI technique, firing if required; 4) pass the light underneath the arm holding the handgun; 5) press the backs of the wrists together, and lower the flashlight-side elbow to increase isometric tension. (Clay Babcock)

come out of the old South West Combat Pistol League—developed the technique that bears his name. Offering recoil control and stability based on Weaver stance principles, the Harries technique has served as the overwhelming choice of handgun/flashlight techniques for armed professionals around the world since it was introduced to the pioneers of practical shooting in Southern California more than two decades ago.

3

4

To employ this technique, the flashlight is held in the nondominant hand with the beam end of the flashlight on the little finger side of the hand. (It may help here to think of a policeman examining a motorist's driver's license at night.) The back of the gun-hand wrist is indexed against the back of the flashlight-hand wrist. Point the flashlight-side elbow toward the ground, not out to the side. Do not simply rest the gun over your flashlight arm. Each hand pulls sideways

5

The Van Keller technique, a reversal of the Harries. The author prefers the standard Harries technique. (Clay Babcock)

against the other to create isometric tension between the backs of the wrists for stability and recoil control.

In assuming this stance, the gun arm is held out first and the flashlight is passed under the gun hand; DO NOT position the light first and pass the pistol over it, or you will sweep your wrist with the muzzle of the gun, violating Jeff Cooper's safety Rule 2: "Never let your muzzle cover anything you are not willing to destroy."

To prevent pointing the gun at yourself when drawing the pistol to the Harries technique, bring the flashlight up to your nondominant-side shoulder à la the aforementioned SFI/CCI technique as you grip the handgun at the beginning of your drawstroke. Then draw and aim your weapon one-handed BEFORE passing the light under your shooting arm. Credit for this idea goes to defensive knife guru Erik Remmen of Northwest Safari, who uses a similar method for transitioning to the handgun after using a knife for weapon retention.

One common mistake with the Harries technique (or any other, for that matter) is to take too much time carefully aligning the beam of the light on the target. As long as there is enough light to identify the target and silhouette the sights, you can fire and hit. Of course, it is still better to put the beam in your adversary's eyes; dry-fire practice is an excellent way to perfect this skill. Note that the Harries is basically a Weaver-stance-only technique, requiring the flashlight arm to be bent more than the gun arm. It will, however, work with lights having either rear or side buttons/switches, and it facilitates a transition to alternate force employment of the flashlight as described in the next chapter.

One variation of the Harries technique, which may have its origins in Canada, is to hold the flashlight-side forearm horizontal (parallel to the ground) and press the gun-hand knuckles into the support arm or wrist for stability. I see no real advantages to this stance, and it is very easy to sweep your arm with the muzzle when assuming it.

A final spin on the Harries is promoted by Georgia State Trooper Van Keller. Instead of passing the light under the gun hand, the flashlight-hand wrist goes over the gun-hand wrist. The resulting stance is more akin to an isosceles than a Weaver and, for me, is less stable than a standard Harries. It also poses the risk of obstructing the slide on a semiauto pistol if not assumed correctly. Additionally, Keller's method is limited to side button flashlights, which must be held with the beam protruding from the thumb side of the hand.

Former FBI Agent Bill Rogers demonstrates the handgun/flashlight technique he developed. (Andy Stanford)

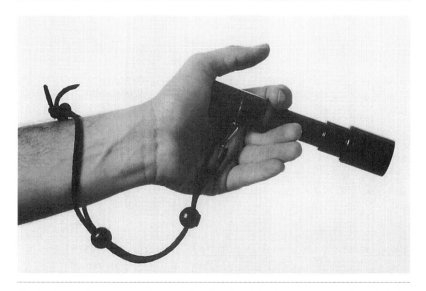

In the Rogers/Sure-Fire technique, the CombatLight from Laser Products is held as shown. The switch is activated by the base of the thumb. (Clay Babcock)

ROGERS/SURE-FIRE TECHNIQUE

Until recently the Harries and Rogers/Chapman techniques were the only flashlight/handgun firing methods that provided recoil control significantly better than one-handed shooting. With the recent introduction of the Laser Products Z ("Zulu") series CombatLights, there is another option that many shooters may find superior, a technique once again attributed to former FBI Agent Bill Rogers.

To use the CombatLight with a Rogers/Sure-Fire technique, the flashlight is held in the nondominant hand with the barrel of the light between the index and middle fingers and the rear button switch against the base of the thumb, somewhat like a syringe. The critical thing here is to be able to turn the light on and off when you want to. The distance between thumb and fingers can be shortened if necessary by removing one or two of the rubber spacers.

The handgun is held in the dominant hand in a standard grip,

The author's favorite hand-held flashlight technique, the Rogers/Sure-Fire, works equally well with either a Weaver or isosceles stance. (Clay Babcock)

then the tips of the lower two or three fingers of the flashlight hand are wrapped around the gun hand in a standard two-handed hold.

This grip allows for the isometric tension that gives the Weaver stance its positive attributes. It works equally well with an isosceles stance.

The primary disadvantage to the Rogers/Sure-Fire technique is that it practically requires the use of a Z-series light. A Sure-Fire 6P can be used—Rogers first developed the technique with this light—but a CombatLight works much better due to the slimmer body diameter, rubber spacers with grip ring, and protruding rear button. Flashlights with a significantly larger-diameter body just won't do, nor will those with other than a protruding rear button switch.

(If you already have a P model Sure-Fire, you can put a piece of bicycle inner tube around the body of the light to provide additional friction; also, with an early P model, you'll need to obtain the newer, protruding switch button from Laser Products. Technique originator Bill Rogers actually prefers this setup to the CombatLight.)

Personally, I find the Rogers/Sure-Fire technique a bit quicker to assume than the Harries, with a higher probability of correctly aligning the CombatLight's beam each time. Additionally, recoil control seems better, and there is little risk of sweeping your wrist with the muzzle when you draw.

Keep in mind, this opinion comes from someone who has used the Harries technique for more than 20 years (Michael was my first combat shooting instructor, in early 1977) so if anything, my biases should be for the older method due to the muscle memory associated with thousands of repetitions. However, even though the Rogers/Sure-Fire method is superior for me, I will continue to teach the Harries technique too, since some people like it better and it works with any switch location.

In fact, it is a good idea to attain a usable degree of proficiency at as many other methods as you can. In certain circumstances, there are advantages to each particular way of shooting with a hand-held light. For example, the FBI technique can be used when entering small rooms to present a false target. The SFI/CCI position is a good way to search without pointing your gun muzzle at everything you illuminate, and it facilitates safe assumption of the Harries, as noted earlier.

Likewise, the Ayoob technique is the quickest way to shoot two-handed when holding your flashlight in a handshake grip with the flashlight beam extending from the thumb side of the hand. Other considerations include how well the technique adapts to less-than-lethal scenarios and malfunction clearances. (The Harries method gets the nod in both respects.) Lastly, note that anytime you have a flashlight in one hand and a firearm in the other, you must be careful to avoid unintentional discharges due to interlimb interaction, or so-called "sympathetic squeeze."

For completeness I should mention that once you have identified a close-range threat when searching with the flashlight, you can simply drop the light and fire with one or both hands. With sufficient practice, it is fairly easy to achieve hits by kinesthetic alignment of weapon and target. However, the obvious downside to this approach is that you have just jettisoned a key piece of night fighting hardware.

IMMEDIATE ACTION TECHNIQUES

When—not if—Murphy's law rears its ugly head in combat, the consequences can be fatal. Hence, you'll need a plan for dealing with situations such as weapon malfunctions and running out of ammo with your primary firearm. In close quarters scenarios, there often won't be time to reload or clear the stoppage. The best course of action will frequently be to transition to your sidearm.

With either a pistol-mounted or hand-held flashlight, you can use your normal transition technique and switch to the sidearm and supplementary illumination tool. Be sure to practice drawing the light at the same time as the pistol if you use a hand-held light. To prevent grabbing the light when you need some other critical piece of kit (e.g., spare magazine), carry each tool in a distinct location.

An alternative is to use the weapon-mounted light on your shoulder weapon to provide illumination for your handgun after you transition. One way to do this is to leave the primary weapon shouldered or tuck it under your nondominant arm. Then draw your handgun and engage as necessary using the light from the shoulder weapon for threat identification and sighting.

Or, if the long gun is equipped with a conventional carry strap—as opposed to a tactical sling—you can sling it muzzle down across your back as taught by Louis Awerbuck of the Yavapai Firearms Academy. Then rotate the muzzle under your nondominant arm and use the weapon-mounted light for illumination while firing with your sidearm.

When you only have a sidearm and hand-held light, you'll need to reload and/or clear malfunctions while maintaining control of the flashlight. Small lights will allow you to perform many operations while still holding onto the flashlight. With a light equipped with a lanyard, you can simply let it dangle from your wrist while you deal with the handgun problem.

If kneeling, wedge the light between your calf and thigh or tuck it into your waistband. Similarly, you can clamp the bezel under your gun-side armpit, pointed to the rear. This will hide the beam in case the light is on, and the non-dominant hand remains free to manipulate magazines, work the slide of an autopistol, etc. Or, if you prefer, clamp it under the support-side armpit to keep the gun hand free. There are pros and cons to each method. Setting the light on the ground is usually not recommended, as it can easily roll away.

A final contingency to consider is: what if you need to use a hand-held light with a shoulder weapon? There are a couple of ways to do this, the first of which is to assume a variation of the Harries technique, passing a hand-held flashlight underneath the long gun. Alternately, hold the light against and parallel to the handguard or fore-end. Neither method is nearly as stable as a weapon-mounted light—probably worse than most handgun/flashlight techniques, too—but either is better than nothing.

You can create a field-expedient, ersatz momentary switch for a hand-held Sure-Fire light (except CombatLights) by adjusting the constant-on switch until the light just barely turns off. Pressing the flashlight against the fore-end will torque the endcap sideways (the head on model 8X), causing the light to turn on; release the pressure and the light goes out. The light can thus be modulated by squeezing and releasing it.

This workaround isn't perfect—sometimes you'll inadvertently rotate the endcap or head a bit as you flex it and the light will stay on—but it does provide a means of momentary switching when using a hand-held Sure-Fire light with a shoulder weapon. This scheme also allows you to use the Ayoob side button handgun technique and momentary switching with a Sure-Fire light.

Whatever method you use for low-light target identification and engagement, practice until it becomes a reflexive action. Skill at arms is primarily a function of time and effort invested in relevant training. Firearms, other fighting implements, ancillary equipment, tactics, and techniques are just tools in your defensive shooting toolbox.

chapter 7

HAND-TO-HAND COMBAT IN LOW LIGHT

A GUN DERIVES ITS SUPERIORITY from its ability to cause damage at a distance. In the absence of ambient light—and lacking night-vision equipment or self-supplied illumination—the visually aimed firearm loses much of this advantage. Samuel Colt may have invented an equalizer, but darkness can change the equation back again.

Before the invention of night vision equipment, prior to the harnessing of electricity, before the development of gunpowder, people fought in low-light conditions. Even today, the situation may arise in which your best option consists of more primitive means of combat.

First of all, any type of equipment can malfunction. Firearms quit due to stoppages or lack of ammo, batteries run out of juice, electronics go "tango uniform," and lamp filaments break. Murphy's law says it will happen at the worst possible moment, and you may have to finish the fight without the benefit of a gun, NVE, or whatever. In addition, proficiency at hand-to-hand combat will develop attributes that are valuable no matter what the lighting conditions.

For these reasons and others, the low-light warrior must become facile in hand-to-hand combat. Where possible, he or she can combine flashlight technology with manufactured fighting tools or body weapons to achieve a synergistic effect. What follows is not intended to be a comprehensive combatives curriculum, but rather to raise several important issues that can guide your training.

USE OF LIGHT CONTINUUM

Before proceeding to physical techniques, let's look at how a flashlight can be used as a nonlethal control tool. One plus to solving things in this manner is the fact that photons do not injure or kill; several attorneys I've spoken with have opined that a mere beam of a light simply cannot constitute excessive force, or any physical force at all for that matter. The physiological and psychological impact of the beam can be modulated to achieve a the desired effect, particularly useful in law-enforcement scenarios.

First of all, if your adversary simply knows you have a flashlight, this could very well affect his actions. The light introduces a variable that is beyond your opponent's control, even if you are not presently shining it directly at him. He can no longer count on the cloak of darkness to conceal his actions. If he has something to hide (e.g., a weapon, contraband), the light will allow you to discover it. Additionally, the real or perceived impact weapon capability of the light can cause further apprehension.

Escalating the use of the light somewhat, you can shine it at your adversary so that no part of the beam is in his eyes. For instance, the light can be used to get a clear look at his hands or waistband. Recall that even peripheral light will destroy dark adaption—his and yours. And shining the beam on anything or anyone close to you can be significantly self-blinding.

To up the ante, shine the peripheral, non-focused part of the beam into your opponent's eyes. This will have a relatively mild physical effect on his vision, and he will still be able to see you. (Cops can use the edge of the beam to perform a roadside pupil check with a flashlight that would otherwise be too bright.)

Cranking things up another notch, the bright, focused area of the beam can be shined directly into his eyes. With anything approaching a high-intensity light, this will cause his eyelids to close forcefully and may even evoke a flinch response. His hands will very likely be used to shield his eyes, which has the positive effect of allowing you to see if he is holding a weapon; on the downside, this reaction will often override other facial expressions, body language, and other important nonverbal cues.

People tend to become disoriented when a powerful light is shined in their eyes, and they may even stop momentarily. These effects are most pronounced when the light is employed without warning. However, be aware that this may provoke a physically violent reaction directed at the source of the irritation (i.e., YOU)!

Finally, you can pulse the bright part of the beam on and off while shining it in your opponent's face. Pulsing the light increases the aggravation factor significantly and is on par with calling his mother a dirty name. The subject may very well lose self-control at this point. Reserve this technique for times when you have decided in advance to lay hands on your opponent and possess the means to deal with the resulting situation—for instance, several large teammates.

You can still affect your opponent's vision significantly while reducing the likelihood of inciting an assault, as follows. Put the focused cone of light into your opponent's eyes for just an instant, then immediately de-escalate to the less intense peripheral part of the beam with a sincere, "Sorry 'bout that." If he doesn't accept your apology, you may have to resort to the methods described below.

EMPTY-HAND TECHNIQUES

When a less-than-lethal level of physical force is required—or if no manufactured fighting tool is available—you may need to resort to unarmed combat. Grappling styles such as jiu-jutsu, wrestling, and shootfighting lend themselves well to the "Braille method" of self-defense in the dark. Throws, submission holds, and joint locks are all applied largely by feel. Indeed, without the requisite level of sensitivity, the arts in question probably won't be effective in a daytime fight. And, obviously, any such techniques can cause crippling injury or death if applied with sufficient vigor.

If you prefer striking instead, you can stay close to your opponent in what jeet kune do practitioners call "trapping range." This is the distance at which elbows, knees, and head-butts can be brought into play. Not only are these extremely powerful strikes, but they are delivered from a proximity that facilitates sensing your adversary's action by feel in low light. You can often keep a checking hand on your opponent as both a control and a monitor and/or maintain contact with his legs in the manner of a silat practitioner. The principle involved is called "adhesion." The unarmed combatives system devised by special forces instructor John Holschen of Insights Training Center uses this approach to good advantage.

Sensitivity drills such as chi sao (from the Chinese art of wing chun) and hubud lubud (from the Philippines) are perfect for honing your tactile reflexes. Blindfolded sparring is also good for developing the ability to respond to nonvisual stimuli. Amazing things can be accomplished with practice: I have seen senior instructors at Modern Warrior Defensive Tactics Institute block kicks and evade throw darts with their vision completely obscured.

Keep in mind that if you can't see well, the ability to deliver visually targeted strikes suffers accordingly. Hitting a small target such as an eyeball or chi meridian from a distance becomes extremely difficult in dim light. Of course, if there is some ambient illumination you're not completely out of business. In fact, since you see with the peripheral rod cells in low light, maintaining the often recommended "soft focus" comes naturally under dusky conditions.

That said, there are inherent risks to employing striking techniques when it is really dark. In the words of Dr. U Maung Gyi, Ghurka combat veteran of WWII and Korea and head of the American Bando Association, "At night it is very easy to slip and fall, or to kick or punch a tree or wall you did not see." It's therefore no surprise that Dr. Gyi recommends the "Python" (grappling) techniques from his art for low-light applications.

A jiu-jutsu master acquaintance of mine who trains special operations personnel describes his job as "teaching eye extractions and chokes." Add the ability to crush a trachea and snap an assailant's neck and you have defined several unarmed low-light force options at the extreme end of the spectrum, right up there with deadly weapons. Each of these techniques can be applied without the need to see the opponent, as can joint locks and breaks.

This is also a good place to bring up strangulation or decapitation by garrote or other flexible weapon, admittedly not an empty-hand technique, but somewhat analogous to a choke. Clearly, use of such a device in a lethal manner by private citizens or law-enforcement officers would be hard to justify in court. It is mentioned here only for completeness, and for consideration by military personnel.

The effects of darkness on unarmed combat go well beyond constraining engagement ranges. Low light can contribute to the success of a technique through concealment of intention and action. The detection of preattack movements—i.e., "telegraphing"— may be more difficult in reduced illumination, depending on the specific light level. On the other hand, as noted previously, rod cells detect movement better than cones, so in this respect low light can actually facilitate quick reactions.

The upshot is that darkness can help the fighter who must rely on his or her empty hands against a person armed with a firearm. For the person skilled in an appropriate fighting system, night can be a powerful ally. Such expertise will come only as the result of extensive training—both general purpose instruction in the art(s) in question, plus task-specific low-light exercises and practice.

THE FLASHLIGHT AS IMPACT WEAPON

Unlike a military special forces operator stalking a sentry, the private citizen or police officer often isn't concerned about remaining unobserved. Hence, in civilian scenarios a flashlight can either be used to temporarily blind your adversary to set up an empty-hand or weapon strike, or be employed as an impact tool in its own right. Exactly how this is done will depend on the type of light you have and how you are holding it.

As mentioned previously, long, heavy aluminum "police flashlights" were intended from the outset for use as makeshift weapons. Cops have been using standard straight baton techniques with flashlights for years. There are several systems taught in academies around the country, from the classic Lamb method to the latest collapsible-baton techniques. John Peters describes a number of workable strikes and blocks in his classic text *Defensive Tactics with Flashlights*.

A Sure-Fire Millennium M1 or 9Z CombatLight can be strapped to the hand for use as an impact tool, as follows: 1) tie a figure-8 knot with the ends of the lanyard, slide both adjusting buttons all the way to the knot, and slip the lanyard over the lamp end of the light, around the back of your hand; 2) cinch down the adjusting bead closest to the light, around the narrow part of the body of the flashlight; 3) slide the second adjusting button next to the one you just moved; 4) loop the excess lanyard around the light and your hand, using the adjusting button farthest from the light to secure the end of the lanyard around your wrist; 5) the light can now be used to visually disable an adversary or to strike with either end or the body of the light. (Clay Babcock)

126

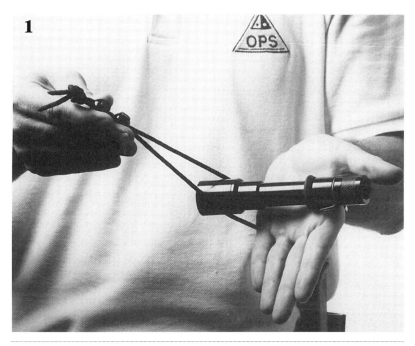

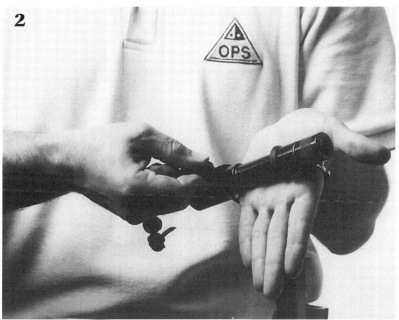

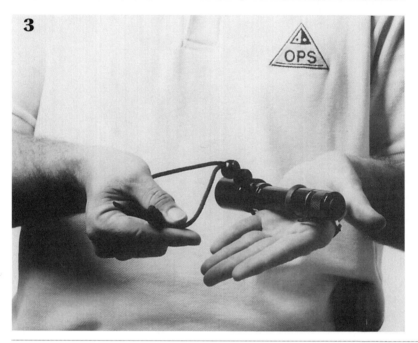

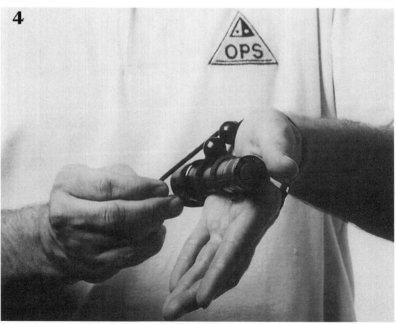

5

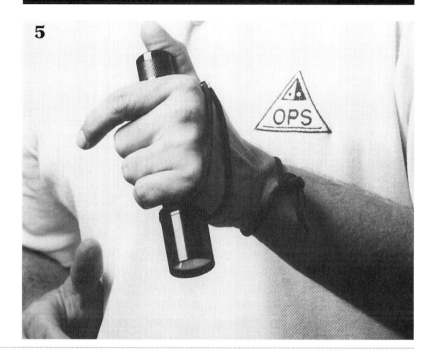

Law-enforcement professionals should obtain some type of documented, formal training in the use of the flashlight in alternate force scenarios. Since the Malice Greene case in Detroit—in which a Motor City police officer beat a suspect to death with a flashlight—many departments have shied away from explicitly addressing the use of this effective defensive tool. However, case law established by *Wellington v. Daniels* (717 F. 2d 932, U.S. Court of Appeals, 1983) states that an agency should either expressly prohibit use of the flashlight as an impact weapon in written policy, or provide adequate instruction in its use. Ignoring the issue is not an option.

As noted in Chapter 4, none of the latest crop of full-sized lights includes tactically optimal switching and beam characteristics. Currently, the best approach for using a light as a full-length night stick is to affix a lamp and reflector to the end of a purpose-built impact weapon. I refer here to the 3- and 6-volt Sure-Fire systems that replace the tailcap on ASP and Casco expandable batons, which feature momentary side switches that can be activated in a standard grip, plus a twist-type constant-on function. ASP also recently introduced a factory baton light, which uses a click-on microprocessor switch on the side. (Recall that click-on switching is suboptimal under stress.)

The Laser Products M1 Millennium CombatLight is a compact alternative that can be carried in a purse or pocket and lends itself well to yawara stick and reverse-grip knife techniques. The Sure-Fire 9Z (lithium) and convertible lithium/Ni-Cd 7Z will also work with the method described next, but the latter has only 50 lumens of light output; the 6Z is usually too short for the technique discussed below, unless you have really small hands. Using the supplied paracord lanyard, the CombatLight can be strapped to your palm as follows.

First tie a figure-8 knot at the end of the supplied lanyard, and slide both adjusting beads to the end of the lanyard farthest from the light. Hold the light so that you can press the tailcap switch with your thumb, then pass the lanyard over the back of your hand. Next, pass the head of the flashlight between the two sides of the lanyard, then cinch the adjusting beads tight. The greater diameter of the flashlight head will prevent the lanyard from sliding off. Finally, loop the excess lanyard around the light and your wrist, and tighten with one of the adjusting beads (see p. 127–129).

Incidentally, there is an easier way: replace the issue lanyard with a suitable length of elastic shock cord. Fastening the light to your hand then becomes a simple matter of stretching the cord over your hand and around the head of the light.

Strikes can then be made with either end of the light—backhand or forehand—while keeping the use of your fingers to eyejab or grapple. The bezel end of the light can be used to hook extremities, as with reverse-grip knife techniques. You can also hit with the side of the light, backed up with your palm, in the fashion of a palm sap. The latter approach may be applied using body mechanics similar to a hook punch, a straight-in thrust, or an overhand "woodpecker" motion. I generally fasten the light

The Sure-Fire CombatLight is well suited to "flash and smash" techniques with a body tool (above, a palm strike), the light itself (left), or some other implement. Note that the light is strapped to the author's non-dominant hand to facilitate the use of a gun or knife. If unarmed or using OC spray, you may wish to strap the light to your dominant hand instead. (Clay Babcock)

to my nondominant hand if carrying a knife or other such weapon, and to my dominant hand if using the flashlight alone or in conjunction with OC "pepper" spray.

A Mini-Mag or similar implement can be used with Kubotan or Persuader key chain techniques. The majority of such lights feature some means of attaching your keys, so even the "flail" strikes from Takayuki Kubota's system can be delivered. Unfortunately, the only switch on most pen lights is a twist-on head, so momentary flashes are basically impossible. (Note, however: if you need to quickly extinguish the beam on a Mini-Mag, simply press the lens against your body.)

The Filipino martial arts—known variously as kali, escrima, or arnis de mano—are an excellent avenue to combat flashlight prowess, no matter what the length of your light. In these South Pacific fighting systems, both offense and defense are based on generic angles of attack that apply to knives, impact tools, or even empty hands. Certain joint locks, too, can be effected with flashlights of any size, as can pressure point techniques.

Use of the flashlight should be coordinated with the timing of your techniques. Attacking no more than a "half beat" after flashing the light in an assailant's eyes will greatly improve your odds of success. With striking arts, the beam will mask the incoming blow. Likewise, an opponent's reflexive response to blinding light will often cause his head to move backwards, thus placing him off balance to facilitate sweeps or throws and enhance their effectiveness.

An impact weapon in the opposite hand can work in concert with the light, reaching out unseen from behind the veiling glare of the beam. A police officer friend of mine has dubbed this approach "flash and smash." One possible tactic here is to flash high, then strike low.

Likewise, you can move to the side while holding the light still or while moving it in the opposite direction. Your assailant will then perceive that you are somewhere other than your true location. The ability to create such illusions is limited only by your imagination and skill.

Whether large, medium, or small, a flashlight can provide capability that goes beyond tactical illumination. Private citizens in particular can benefit from carrying an implement that is legal in most jurisdictions and locations that prohibit weapons per se. I have personally carried a Sure-Fire CombatLight in courthouses, on commercial airliners, and overseas without any hassle whatsoever from those in charge.

EDGED WEAPONS

Darkness can be a great ally to the person who carries an edged weapon. An old swordsman's adage holds, "Let your enemy feel your steel before he sees it." Similarly, Hwa Rang Do martial artist and Warrior knife designer Bob Taylor opines, "In self-defense, a knife is not used to threaten, 'go away or I'll cut you,' but rather, 'go away or I'll cut you . . . again!'" Darkness can assist you in achieving the element of surprise, both strategic and tactical.

One essential skill for nighttime use of a folding knife is the ability to prevent the signature "click" when the knife is opened. Since hearing becomes more acute in low light due to the lack of visual cues, eliminating the noise of opening can be critical to achieving the aforementioned element of surprise.

A lockback folder with a center lock can be easily and completely muted through the application of pressure on the lock bar as the blade is brought into battery—or even just holding it tightly as taught by Northwest Safari President Eric Remmen—and will still lock positively every time.

In contrast, a liner lock is relatively difficult to silence completely, whatever its technical merits. Not only does quieting a liner lock require fine motor skills that may disappear under stress, attempting to do so will often prevent the lock from moving fully into position, compromising safety. Nonetheless, liner locks are very popular these days, and muting these knives is not impossible.

To stealthily open a liner lock, my colleague Mike Janich—author of *Knife Fighting: A Practical Course* and *Street*

A Spyderco Endura used in conjunction with a Sure-Fire 9Z CombatLight to effect a "flash and slash." Note the elevation change, targeting the area between the opponent's legs. In low light the now visually disabled adversary would have little idea as to the location of the flashlight-bearing defender. (Clay Babcock)

Steel: Choosing and Carrying Self-Defense Knives—recommends using the middle finger to prevent the lock from snapping open, then manually pushing the liner into position. Another workable method of quietly deploying a liner lock is to thumb the blade most of the way open, then use your first slash to complete opening it . . . against your foe's body.

As with empty-hand fighting, desirable techniques for edged-weapon combat in darkness are largely a function of reduced visibility. Remember, in low light your eyesight drops below a level equivalent to being legally blind. Precise thrusts may be out of the question. There are a couple of alternative strategies to achieving success when you can't see well. Each can be optimized through choice of hardware.

At night, sticking to your assailant like glue constitutes a method of knife fighting akin to grappling; the aforementioned Warrior knife is perfect for this strategy. Another approach when you can't see well is to use a heavy, fairly long blade (e.g., Kukri, Bowie, sword) and rely primarily on chopping motions. Just remember: whether in a military or civilian scenario, it's not a good idea to cut anyone you haven't positively identified as hostile. Decapitating a shadowy figure carries the risk of beheading a buddy or bystander.

You may wish to augment your edged weapon with a hand-held flashlight, as described above. Filipino stylists can use espada y daga movements, adjusting as necessary for the increased inertia of the heavy light compared to a rattan escrima stick when a full-sized flashlight is used. The CombatLight short stick techniques discussed previously work well too. The beam can distract your assailant and conceal the movements of the knife, working in synergy with the blade.

Such techniques harken back to the old "lantern and dagger" methods of yore. The ultimate evolution of the "flash and slash" concept may be an integration of cutting and illumination equipment into one package. We've already seen utility knives like the Spyderco Firefly that combine a blade and a light. Mating a high-intensity, impact-resistant flashlight to a task-specific edged weapon would result in a highly effective self-defense tool. Any designers out there interested in advancing the state of the art?

Whatever the gear you employ, understand that equipment ranks fourth behind mind-set, tactics, and skill in the hierarchy of survival factors. The next two chapters will discuss esoteric low-light tactics and the training required to hone your skill at fighting in low light.

8

LOW-LIGHT TACTICS

THE WORD "TACTICS," along with its adjective form "tactical," has become quite a popular buzzword of late. While perfectly valid when used appropriately, these terms are all too often commandeered for marketing purposes to convey an unspecified military mystique.

So what exactly do we mean by tactics? The root of the word, *tact*, is Greek, meaning touch. Contrast this with strategy, from the Greek *strat*, which means "to general." Strategy is the guiding philosophy at the highest level, tactics are the decisions and actions that execute the strategy in a tangible manner, and techniques are the basic physical building blocks.

My favorite definition of tactics—from Webster via former Secret Service agent and fellow National Tactical Invitational Shotist Gary Wistrand—is, *The art or science of using the available means to achieve an end.* In other words, tactics are the actions you take in furtherance of your particular goal, with your options frequently constrained by the mission, opponent(s), resources, environment, and time available.

Another good definition comes from Mas Ayoob: *Common sense applied with the specific knowledge of the involved discipline.* In this case the discipline in question is fighting under conditions of reduced illumination. The chapters in this book contain some of the specific knowledge you'll need. Supplying the common sense, that oh-so-uncommon virtue, is up to you. Tactical acumen is largely a matter of decision-making under stress.

You can also think of tactics as tools in a toolbox. Picking the right one for the job is important; employing a hammer when a saw is needed just won't cut it. On the other hand, intelligent use of tactics can provide "leverage" in a confrontation, allowing you to accomplish things far out of proportion to the effort expended. Having a wide range of tactics at your disposal maximizes the probability that you will select a suitable course of action.

In reading what follows, you'll notice that I frequently use such words as "often," "might," and "probably," avoiding cut-and-dried pronouncements of what you should or should not do. The actions you can take to solve a particular problem will vary with the situation. It would be presumptuous and irresponsible for me to give you cookbook recipes for solving tactical situations about which I do not have first-hand knowledge—ones in which I personally face no risk of death, injury, or legal consequences.

Lastly, be aware that virtually everything you can do will involve a trade-off. Whether the pros of a particular tactic outweigh the cons is a decision you'll have to make based on the information available at the time. Tactics is often more art than science, and there are never any guarantees.

STAPLE TACTICS

Just because a confrontation occurs at night doesn't mean that all daytime tactics go out the window. Several important principles are equally valid regardless of the lighting conditions. It is worth examining some of the most com-

Normal daytime tactics, such as use of cover and concealment, should still be employed in a low-light confrontation. (Ichiro Nagata, PDC)

mon general tactical guidelines to see how they might change in low light.

Use Cover and Concealment Wherever You Can

Cover stops bullets; concealment merely hides you from view. People tend to get lax about using actual cover in low light, since they are often concealed by the darkness. Just because you can't be seen doesn't mean you can't be shot! Still, concealment is better than nothing, and as we shall see shortly, the lower the light level, the greater the tactical flexibility you will have.

In any case, be careful not to shine a light against any object directly in front of you, as the beam can bounce back, illuminating and/or blinding you; this caution also applies to windows, which typically reflect around 5 percent of light hitting them, not to mention mirrors.

139

Maximize Distance Between Yourself and Potential Threat Areas

This principle generally applies when you are using a firearm, since distance favors the skilled shooter. As noted in the previous chapter, low light levels even the odds between those with guns and those who are unarmed or wielding a contact weapon, due a corresponding reduction in engagement ranges. (If you are the one without a gun, you can employ the inverse principle and close with your adversary.) In any case, distance equates to time, which may be sorely needed at night due to slower decision-making ability. Thus the closer distances typical of night fighting exacerbate this problem.

Don't Turn Your Back on Anything You Haven't Checked

Darkness impacts this principle in a couple of ways. First of all, thoroughly searching a given location becomes more difficult as light levels decrease. This is due both to areas of shadow, plus the finite size of a light beam or NVE field of view. Secondly, it is easier in the dark for an assailant to slip unnoticed into a previously searched area. (During the daytime the ability to circle around is limited primarily by tangible impediments.) For these reasons and more, you shouldn't regard any area not under your immediate control as free from hostile individuals.

Move to Your Adversary's Flanks When Possible (and Guard Your Own)

Low light levels can help you to execute this tactic, but you are more susceptible to being outflanked as well. The tunnel vision that occurs as a result of the human fight-or-flight response is exacerbated by the aforementioned limits of a flashlight beam or NVE field of view. With multiple assailant confrontations on the rise, the likelihood of being attacked from more than one direction is greater than ever.

During team operations, light can facilitate flanking your opponent(s). One or more team members can use high intensity illumination to distract and visually disable the subject(s), while other team members maneuver to the flanks outside of the beam. This tactic can be used with firearms and also facilitates less lethal takedowns and control holds. The other guy won't even see it coming, and hence cannot prepare to resist. (In an arrest situation, the "light man" can verbalize "look toward my voice" or otherwise distract the subject with conversation.)

Employ Sound Target Engagement Procedures

When using force against an aggressor, your survival depends on your actions before, during, and after the application of physical techniques. Unfortunately, many people drop their guard before it is safe to do so. A failure to follow through appropriately can get a person killed in short order. Fortunately, the problem has been studied and solutions derived.

The general procedure is as follows: fight (until the threat appears neutralized); do I have to fight anymore? (assess whether your adversary is really out of commission); do I have to fight anyone else? (scan all areas not under control for additional threats); prepare to fight again (if using a firearm, reload, from behind cover if possible).

Low light levels can affect each of these steps. Fighting can be more difficult in conditions of reduced illumination. A wounded assailant can play possum more easily in low light, or disappear into the darkness. Scanning for accomplices is more difficult and less certain in the dark, and it gives away your location. And weapon manipulations may be hindered by the need to hold onto low-light tools.

"Always Cheat—Always Win"

Thunder Ranch Director Clint Smith came up with this phrase to list the only two rules that apply in a violent confrontation. The concept dovetails well with that of ruthlessness, one of Jeff Cooper's Principles of Personal Defense from the book of the same name. Darkness will assist you in fighting "unfairly." With your actions concealed by conditions of reduced illumination, it is that much easier to be sneaky. As will be discussed shortly, a low light environment provides a blank canvas upon which you can paint any number of illusions.

Understand that the above only scratches the surface of this topic. One could devote a lifetime of study to tactics and still not know everything. Nonetheless, if you apply the above guidelines consistently and skillfully, the odds of survival will increase in your favor. Combining these general principles with the esoteric low-light tactics discussed next, you can often gain an overwhelming advantage.

READING THE LIGHT

The environment in which you fight will frequently influence your tactical decisions. For example, in an outdoor military scenario, evaluating the terrain facilitates movement of forces onto the high ground or other positions of advantage. (The outcome of the pivotal Civil War battle at Gettysburg, PA, was largely due to an astute assessment of the topography by cavalry General John Buford, the first Union commander on scene.)

Likewise, in low-light scenarios, individuals and teams will benefit immensely if they can instantly characterize the lighting conditions in the area of operations. In fact, the ability to prevail during a confrontation in reduced illumination or darkness is largely a function of how well the parties involved take advantage of the ambient lighting, employing the tools previously discussed as available and appropriate.

Of course, light levels can vary infinitely from the pitch black at the bottom of a deep mine shaft to the flash of a nuclear explosion. These can be quantified by a light meter if necessary. Common units of measure include lux (metric) and foot candles. See the chart in Chapter 1 for typical values. However, for tactical purposes the amount of light at a given location can be classified into one of the following four general categories:

BRIGHT. An intense light source that is detrimental to your eyesight. That is, bright light impairs the ability to see, and, if strong enough to result in veiling glare, may prevent vision entirely.

MEDIUM. In medium light, you can see detail and color and can perceive depth. This range of light levels provides enough illumination for human photopic (cone) vision. In short, you can see well enough to perform the task at hand.

LOW. For our purposes, low lighting comprises those conditions under which lack of illumination negatively impacts eyesight, depriving you of the information you need to make decisions. You may still see certain objects, in silhouette if nothing else, and particularly those that move.

NONE. Self-explanatory. In such an environment you cannot see anything without the aid of some type of low-light tool. Generally this condition occurs only inside a manmade or natural structure (e.g., a cave), since even at night the sky provides some illumination.

The level of light you perceive will vary with your dark adaption. For instance, automobile headlights at a distance may seem blindingly bright at night, but not during daytime. Likewise, if you move from a light area to a significantly darker one, it may initially seem that there is no light at all, but after a short while you will be able to discern silhouettes or even coarse detail.

The effects of a given light source—whether ambient (i.e., present independent of any illumination tools employed) or self-supplied—will vary with its position relative to you, your team members (if any), and your opponent(s). You need to think in terms of what the other guy is seeing.

What you don't see CAN hurt you. This "dark hole" conceals an armed adversary. (J.C. Ponce)

Of particular interest is "bad" lighting, here meaning not insufficient illumination, but rather lighting conditions that militate against your goals. There are three primary types of bad lighting, as follows:

BLINDING FRONT LIGHT. The classic example of this condition is the fighter pilot attacking out of the sun. Or, an earlier version: a Samurai jockeying for advantageous position would often strike upon feeling the sun on the back of his neck, since at that point his opponent couldn't see to defend against the blow. In low light or darkness, high-intensity artificial illumination can easily produce a similar effect.

BACKLIGHTING. Any light source behind you can silhouette you, betraying your presence. Since rod cells are designed to pick up movement, even extremely low levels of backlighting can facilitate detection by an adversary. (A light background can produce a similar effect.) Remember: while you must identify what you are shooting at, your adversary has no such restrictions and can fire indiscriminately at shapes and sounds!

DARK HOLES. These are poorly lit areas into which you cannot see without the aid of a low-light tool. All dark holes represent a potential threat until you determine otherwise. This is simply a low-light version of the previously mentioned tactical principle, "Don't turn your back on anything you haven't checked."

The bad news is that these three unequal lighting conditions can put you at a serious disadvantage. The good news is that with an appropriate illumination tool—flashlight, firearms light mount, spotlight—the environment can often be altered in your favor, provided you are "light aware."

TACTICAL ILLUMINATION

Having identified the lighting conditions, you can then apply light or refrain from doing so to achieve a given purpose. Make no mistake: a light is a significant weapon unto itself. Having a suitable light is analogous to being able to change the weather. You may not always be able to completely negate "bad" lighting, but you can usually improve the odds. Achieving this requires that the device be used in a tactically sound manner.

Don't assume that your daytime tactics will work in the dark by simply adding a flashlight. For instance, consider the staple building-clearing technique of systematically searching a room via incremental radial movement, commonly called "slicing the pie." In sufficient ambient light in an environment that does not betray your presence with shadows and/or reflections you can often locate an adversary before he sees you. However, if you simply perform the same procedure at night with a light you will telegraph both your location and your next move via the beam—even if you turn the light off after checking a given "slice."

Similarly, turning the light on continuously when navigating or searching has a serious downside, especially if your beam cannot illuminate the entire area of interest. Doing so will generally alert your adversary as to your exact position and direction of travel, making you an easy target.

Yes, there are times to turn the light on for an extended period. For instance, when you have located a potential assailant and are engaging him verbally or with force, you will often maximize the odds by shining the light in his eyes while you resolve the problem. Or in a confined space that can be entirely lit up by your light (e.g., a bathroom), you can see everything in one fell swoop. Lastly, if you have sufficient cover, manpower, and lighting tools, you can illuminate a given area while maneuvering behind the "wall of light" effect. Police officers have been doing this for decades with vehicle lighting.

Some hostage rescue teams switch on their weapon-

Even a low level of backlighting can betray your presence. Here, an entry team has been silhouetted in the doorway as they move through this "fatal funnel." (Sure-Fire Institute)

Blinding front light will place anyone on the receiving end at a distinct disadvantage. As shown here, a high-intensity beam is a force to be reckoned with even during the daytime. (Ichiro Nagata, PDC)

149

mounted lights for the duration of the assault phase of an operation. These HRTs depend on speed, surprise, and violence of action to overwhelm their opponents during dynamic clearing, which potentially offsets the drawback to constant-on employment. Unfortunately, low light tends to slow things down and constant illumination telegraphs the operator's location and direction of travel. Hence, speed and surprise are impacted. Likewise, discriminate violence becomes more difficult under artificial illumination.

In furtherance of such an operation, pyrotechnic distraction devices—aka flash-bang or flash-crash grenades—can also affect a subject's vision. Producing momentary illumination of 1 million candela or more (a typical camera flash equals 50,000 candela), plus one hell of a loud noise, flash-bang usage is enhanced by the uncertainty and fear that darkness brings.

Getting back to flashlights, in many situations additional advantage can be gained by using lights briefly, intermittently, and unpredictably. It is also a good idea to change the height at which the light appears when possible; this adds to the uncertainty experienced by your opponent, who should perceive nothing more than a chaotic light show. When illuminating, occasionally shine the beam in a random direction to further confuse your enemy.

It is generally desirable to change location relative to the most likely threat axis after turning the light off. You should also move after discharging a firearm, since muzzle flash will also betray your position. By so doing, the only information you have given your adversary is your *previous* location, which is an illusion. Hence, he will tend to make bad decisions based on outdated intelligence.

The basic rule is: the more light behind you—or directly on you—the more light you should apply. I have seen this rendered as, "If you are in the light, use your light; if you are in the dark, leave it dark." But this oversimplifies the matter. For sure the three "bad" lighting conditions listed above are good candidates for a healthy dose of photons, unless there is some reason to leave the light off. You can counter a blinding front light in kind, blind or confuse someone who sees you in backlight (no need to leave the light off since they already know where you are), and/or shine your beam into a dark hole to locate anyone hiding there and destroy their dark adaption. Control the light; control the fight.

Note that achieving any of these effects requires that the light be sufficiently powerful for the conditions. Relatively weak alkaline lights are almost never enough. Even the brightest Gen III light may not provide enough illumination with a general-purpose beam for wide-open spaces such as warehouses. This is where extended range reflectors or larger spotlights come into their own. Also, the more ambient light present, the less effect to be realized from self-supplied illumination.

A light can be used too much or too little. In the first instance you continually give your current position away. In the second, an adversary can move unseen into an area that was previously "cleared" with the beam. Use the light in a manner that will appear random to an observer, at the optimum rate for the lighting conditions.

The last sentence begs the question: what is the optimum rate? This is probably impossible to describe in print, and in any case must be learned through trial and error in training. Nonetheless, per the above guideline, you will want to use the light sparingly in extremely low light. When it is very dark, don't turn the light on unless you need it to navigate, search, or engage a threat. On the other hand, if you are backlit or otherwise visible you aren't fooling anyone, and so can only gain by using the light against your opponent.

Extremely rapid "strobing" of the light —i.e., flashflashflashflashflash—will accomplish little more than continuous-on use, except perhaps to draw the opponent's attention to you. In most cases there should be a distinct, irregular interval during which the light is completely off, though this period can be very short if necessary. You can see why momentary switching capability is so important.

Countering the adverse effects of a light aimed at you can be accomplished in a couple ways. First of all, you can raise your own weapon and/or light to eye level, thereby blocking some of the incoming beam. Or you can tip your head down, shielding your eyes with your brow; a hat with a brim provides additional capability in this regard. Looking low with your eyes in shadow will allow you to gain at least some information about the nature of the threat, e.g., number and location of adversaries, etc.

All of these tactics should be augmented with certain standard operating procedures. Flashlights used in high-risk scenarios should have fresh batteries. (Partially depleted cells can be used in training, but only if you make absolutely sure there is no way they will end up on active duty.) Carrying "reload" batteries is also a practical option with today's smaller cells, but changing them takes time. Hence, as noted before you should always carry at least two lights, one of which is a lithium-powered model. Wearing one or more of these on your person will ensure that illumination is always available.

PSYCHOLOGICAL TACTICS

A person's behavior during a confrontation can be described by the acronym OODA: Observe, Orient, Decide, Act. Low light levels affect each stage of the cycle. Observation becomes more difficult or even impossible, leading to an inability to orient to the problem accurately, even when the opponent is not explicitly using deception Decisions tend to be arrived at more slowly and are less likely to be based on correct input. The resulting actions are often suboptimal, to say the least.

The previously described tactics will interfere with the ability of your adversary to complete the OODA cycle, making him unable to respond in a timely manner or even causing him to pause altogether. Additionally, with practice your OODA cycle will occur much more quickly than his, forcing him to play "catch up" in an ever-worsening spiral. Inevitably, he will lose the fight. Proactive use of lighting tools can hasten his downfall.

Self-supplied illumination can be used to accomplish three things. A powerful light can: 1) allow you to see, which facilitates navigation, searching, shooting, and so on; 2) prevent your adversary from seeing; and/or 3) control the actions of your adversary. Certainly #2 will help you to accomplish #3, but the third attribute goes far beyond a blindingly bright beam, and it is the least understood attribute of tactical illumination.

An old martial arts adage states, "If I can control your body I can win half of the time, but if I can control your mind for a fraction of a second, I can win every single engagement." A high-intensity light gives you the ability to control both your assailant's body—i.e., his primary sensor, the eyes—and his mind, by allowing him to see only what you want him to see.

One primary way of misleading an assailant is to feint in a particular direction by flashing the light several times while moving, then change course and double back in the dark. Be aware that a high intensity lamp will glow for an instant after the switch is turned off, tracing your path if you are moving. (Of course, you can use this to your advantage as well.)

You can also limit your adversary's movement. Most aggressors are loath to move from darkness into the light. Hence, the beam can be used to fence off a particular area. Even if the individual hiding there bolts, you will have a clear indication of his presence and direction of travel, and have an opportunity to engage him with gunfire if this is required.

Similarly, you can use powerful illumination to drive your adversary into the darkness—where other team members are waiting to engage him using NVE. The British Special Air Service frequently used this tactic a decade or so ago during their unrestrained war on the Irish Republican Army.

One tactic that has been recommended in the past is to roll your flashlight into a room. There are a couple of possible problems here. First of all, you have just lost control over both switching and where the light is pointed. (The light could very well end up aimed back at you.) Additionally, you have separated yourself from a valuable piece of gear, and retrieving it provides your adversary with a great opportunity to assault you.

I won't say never set the light down, but understand the ramifications clearly before proceeding, especially if you are committing your one and only light to this tactic. Obviously, if you carry a second light as (strongly) recommended, and/or if you have beaucoup illumination-toting backup, you have more flexibility in this regard.

Opening doors is one situation where grounding a flashlight might make sense. Aim the light at the doorway, then turn the door handle from a position off to one side. Placing the light on top of an object above ground level will prevent the beam from being obstructed by rough terrain and will look more like a person holding a light, for deception purposes.

Speaking of doors, it is generally a good idea to close them behind you when moving through a structure. Not only does this minimize the degree of backlighting suffered due to the doorway, it also will provide an audible indication of an adversary who has gone undetected or circled around behind you.

Another specialized lighting technique is to bounce the light around an obstacle, casting the shadow of anyone hiding behind it onto a nearby wall. Clearly this requires a particular structural geometry, plus a light-colored surface to reflect the beam. However, one situation in which this frequently works is in checking whether someone is hiding in a rest room stall by standing on the toilet: shine the light at the floor underneath the door, and observe the resulting shadows on the ceiling.

A final thought: consider using your flashlight even under daylight conditions. A high-intensity beam can still affect your assailant's vision in fairly strong light, particularly at close range. Even if it does not blind him, he may think, for just an instant, "What the hell . . . ?" The resulting effect on his mind may slow his reflexes and provide just the edge you need to win.

The preceding should not be considered a comprehensive list of lighting tactics. The art of using light—especially man-portable devices such as weapon-mounted lights—to achieve defensive and tactical goals is in its infancy. Use what is here as a starting point from which to develop your own procedures. Who knows? You may make a significant contribution to the field.

OPERATING IN THE DARK

Today's professional illumination tools give users unprecedented options for winning encounters in dim light and darkness. But applying artificial illumination is not the answer to every low-light tactical problem. For instance, a flashlight will not penetrate smoke or fog, and using a light in such cloudy environments can actually make it harder for you to see, while pinpointing your location for your adversary. Perhaps more importantly, in situations in which you want to remain undetected, turning on a high-intensity beam will instantly defeat said goal. When stealth is the objective, darkness becomes a valuable ally.

Of course, to use darkness, it helps if it's actually dark. This sounds obvious, but as you know by now, there is dark and then there is DARK. If you have any choice in the matter, plan the date and time of your operation to minimize ambient light. Examples of such periods include nights with a new moon and early morning hours in urban and suburban areas.

Similarly, choose a route that avoids known light sources and populated areas whenever possible. In some cases, you may be able to modify ambient lighting to your advantage. Electric lighting at the objective can be extinguished either by cutting the power or shooting out the lamp(s) with a sound-suppressed firearm.

Significantly reduced illumination greatly increases the probability that you can apply one of the most important principles of warfare and personal defense: surprise. Darkness facilitates undetected tactical maneuvers, allowing you to move to a position from which you can challenge or strike without warning.

In achieving this objective, light discipline is critical. In even a moderately dark area, a white light "unintentional discharge" will alert everyone within line of sight to your presence. Test your lights far in advance of your jump-off point. Some weapon-mounted lights can be purchased with a switch system that includes a "disable" function, a feature I highly recommend. An opaque pop-open lens cover accomplishes the same thing on either weapon-mounted or handheld flashlights. Ordnance tape over the lens can provide a makeshift alternative.

If you must use illumination while remaining relatively covert—for example, to navigate—you can cover the lens of your high intensity light with a pop-open lens cover with a pinhole in the center. I have also seen a long cylindrical lens cover used by the Border Patrol to limit peripheral light while tracking illegal aliens and smugglers at night. With either approach, aim the light downward to limit your signature.

To illuminate for reading maps and such when your opponent may be equipped with a night vision device, I recommend using a Mini-Mag light with red filter, covered with a piece of electrical tape with a pin hole. Cover yourself completely with a heavy poncho or shelter half, and have teammates sit on the edges to prevent any leakage of light. To test how effectively you can execute this procedure, experiment with the technique while having a partner observe with night vision equipment.

The probability that your adversary will possess NVE is much greater now than in the past. Clues that you may be facing such high-tech equipment include lights off when they should be on. An adversary equipped with NVE may adjust the device, disclosing its presence. And an individual walking while wearing NVGs may extend his hands forward, feeling for obstacles due to loss of depth perception.

If you have your own image intensification device, you

will be able to clearly see any active IR illuminator and may be able to detect the glow of the adversary's device against his face. Additionally, when a night vision scope is aimed directly at you, a glow will often be visible through your own NVE due to retroreflectivity. Lastly, some Russian night vision devices produce electromagnetic interference that might be detected via a radio receiver.

In case you haven't figured this out on your own: don't smoke. This will betray you by both the glow and the smell and, as noted in Chapter 1, can detrimentally affect your ability to dark adapt.

Stay to the shadows whenever you can, moving to the area with the lowest level of light. Do not cross open areas unless you lack an alternate route or have some other over-riding reason to do so. Stay below the horizon to avoid back-lighting. When stationary, kneel or lie down. For the same reason, look around objects instead of over them. When operating around or inside of a structure, realize that you can be backlit against windows and doorways, plus by light coming through cracks under or around doors, etc.

Reflections can also give you away. Shiny gear has no place in a high-risk situation, day or night. Eyeglasses and optics are one potential source of glint that you may not be able to eliminate, but which you should cover when possible. The objective lens of a large night vision device is a particu-larly egregious offender. Antireflective coatings can both improve light transmission and decrease shine. Use of a hon-eycombed antireflection device like the Tenabrex Kill Flash will also help.

To preserve your night vision, you must avoid exposure to white light as much as possible. If you need to read or see to perform a particular task, use a red filter on your flash-light. When deploying from a vehicle, rig red interior light-ing when available. With adjustable dashboard lighting, turn the rheostat to its lowest setting. As noted in Chapter 1, wearing sunglasses during the day can also increase your ability to dark-adapt.

On the same topic, remember that using night vision equipment will destroy your dark adaption. Ideally, all personnel on a team will have the same maximum degree of capability. If only one person has night vision, the device should probably be employed in a scouting or observation role. Then, use ambient and/or self-supplied white light for the entry, raid, or assault. In fact, it's a good idea to use a diverse range of gear, since each type of equipment has its unique strengths and weaknesses and may be unuseable in certain environments and/or under specific lighting conditions.

Noise discipline is also of paramount importance. You simply must eliminate all unwanted sounds. A good place to start is with a preoperations noise abatement check. Do a forward roll, or jump up and down, while another person listens for any sound other than the rustle of clothing and the impact of your body against the ground. Locate the source of the noise and muffle it or get rid of it.

Carry only what you absolutely need and leave everything else behind (for instance, equipment that is only of use in the daylight). The more stuff you have with you, the greater the probability that someone will hear you. Metallic noises are invariably human in origin, and experienced listeners will not mistake them for anything else. Ergo, it is critical to eliminate all potential for this type of sound. Practice disengaging weapon safety catches without a telltale "click." Velcro is another common offender; use some other kind of closure if at all possible.

Tape or otherwise silence equipment such as sling swivels which may clatter against other objects. Physically isolate the offending gear with cloth, tape, or some other baffle if necessary. Pouches that carry multiple ammunition magazines in the same compartment are particularly bad in this respect; a design with individual pockets should be used instead when possible. If you must use the 3-mag nylon GI M-16 pouch, the magazines themselves can be muffled by slipping a two-inch piece of inner tube around them near the floorplate.

Don't fiddle with your gear unnecessarily. If you set something down—e.g., a weapon, night vision viewer, etc.—position it as best you can then leave it alone until you need it next. (To prevent losing mission-essential equipment in the dark, "dummy cord" all critical items to your person with a 550 paracord lanyard approximately as long as your arm.) Similarly, when you settle into a position, get as comfortable as possible so you won't have to shift around.

Movement is a another potential source of trouble, from both a visual and auditory standpoint. Since the rod cells of the retina pick up movement, you should step smoothly and steadily. Jerky motion does not blend with the natural environment and will be interpreted by the brain accordingly. Some primitive tribesmen are very adept at synchronizing their movements with nature, for instance swaying with the wind like a small tree; you may not ever achieve this level of stealth, but it is possible.

To minimize the noise you make when moving, walk slowly and deliberately. Initial contact with the ground should be made with either your toe or the side of your foot. Evaluate the surface in question before settling your weight. If you are about to tread on an object you suspect will make noise when stepped upon (e.g., a dry twig or leaf), either scoot it aside or shift your foot to another location. Set your foot down very gradually, rolling slowly onto the sole. If wading through a stream or river, place your foot with a downstream motion to eliminate splash.

On missions where you must ingress stealthily against a time deadline, move more quickly in the beginning, reducing your rate of travel as you near the objective. As a corollary for military personnel on hit-and-run missions, once you have achieved your objective you can egress rapidly in the resulting commotion. (If the enemy are all dead, it's still okay to haul ass initially!) Then, after you have put some distance between yourself and your dirty work, slow the pace down.

Reconnaissance can go a long way toward eliminating unwanted sounds. The more familiar you are with the terrain, the easier you can avoid potentially noisy obstacles or circumvent a threat altogether. If you are fighting on your own turf, so much the better.

When deployed to a given locale for an extended period, seek to exploit your home court advantage to the maximum possible extent. You will want to become completely familiar with your area of operation, including man-made infrastructure, trails, macro and micro terrain features, nocturnal noises, and vegetation patterns. With an intimate understanding of the environment, tactical activities can be conducted much more quickly and quietly.

For the same reasons, when time permits and sufficient intelligence about the objective is available, mission- and location-specific rehearsals should be conducted. The DeSantis holster company manufactures a set of goggles that simulate low light levels and will allow for daytime practice of some nighttime skills. Still, there is no substitute for putting in many hours of actual low-light training.

Of course some actions will result in noise no matter what you do. When this is the case, take advantage of any ambient sounds—for instance, passing vehicles—to mask your own. And realize that it's not a perfect world. At times, the best you can do is to minimize your audible signature. For instance, if you and your teammates are moving through dry leaves or brush, the point man can clear a path through the offending fauna by shuffling his feet, allowing those that follow to move more quietly.

Since stealth is a staple night-fighter attribute, learned largely through actual on-the-ground experience, suitable training should be a priority. For starters, have a third-party observer evaluate how silently you operate, both when you are still and when you are moving. This is especially important when you are working with a group, since the little sounds made by individual team members very quickly add up. In troubleshooting your noise discipline, the first thing to try is slowing down your rate of movement.

When operating in the dark, use all of your senses. Since the vision you normally depend on is largely gone, depend on your ears to a much greater degree. What you think you hear will often be more reliable than what you think you see.

Similarly, trust your instincts. Humans continuously receive a large amount of sensory input from a wide variety of sources. You can take this discussion as far out as you want to, but even if we limit it to scientifically verified phenomena, you won't necessarily be consciously aware of everything that is going on around you. The bottom line is: if you get a bad feeling about something, it may well be the result of valid input that has been processed subconsciously.

TEAM TACTICS

Whether operating covertly without light or using tactical illumination to search and engage, operating with more than one person greatly improves your odds. The number of tactical options available increases dramatically when additional guns can be brought to bear. In the words of Dave Maynard of the Sure-Fire Institute, "One equals one; two equals four."

To achieve this type of synergy requires that team members operate in concert, as opposed to each person doing his or her own thing. At a minimum this means achieving the three "C"s: Cover all potential threat areas (visually and/or with weapons); Coordinate movement toward a common goal; and Communicate with team members to achieve the first two Cs. Otherwise, all you've got is a bunch of individuals fighting alone together!

Each of these three actions generally becomes more difficult in low light. We already know that situational awareness is severely degraded in dim or dark environments. Covering large areas is just that much harder when you can't use your normal daytime eyesight. The good news is that each additional pair of eyes and ears, night-vision device, or illumination tool greatly improves the situation compared with operating solo.

The ability to communicate with team members can also suffer due to lack of illumination, particularly when stealth is critical. First of all, unless you are equipped with NVE, visual hand signals will be useless in many low-light situations. To effect command and control, team leaders can physically move members in a given direction. A squeeze of the hand can be used for simple messages like "yes" or "no," but significantly more complicated messages frequently cannot be conveyed via such symbolic language. At a static location (e.g., ambush site) a length of sturdy cord can be passed among team members, then used to alert them via tugs on the line.

Radio transceivers should be equipped with an earplug or bone vibration speaker. (If this is not possible, you will need to be extremely careful to turn the volume down or the device off as necessary.) Coded messages can be transmitted via "dead carriers" by keying push-to-talk microphones, e.g., one click yes, two clicks no.

You may have no choice but to talk, which can disclose your presence and location. When communicating verbally, the "sender" should stand close and whisper directly into the ear of the "receiver" while the latter maintains coverage of his or her threat areas. And remember, a garbled message may be worse than none at all. To reduce the risk of misunderstanding, it is imperative that you follow the ABCs of tactical communication—Accuracy, Brevity, and Clarity.

That said, the effect of low light on communication isn't all bad. When employing tactical illumination techniques, your flashlight can convey explicit or implicit information all its own. You can use the light to signal, with or without a colored filter; just understand that you will inevitably disclose your position by doing so. Some units used different colored lens covers to designate different squads/teams and to identify friend and foe. Also, the beam can point out such things as direction of travel or threat locations. Similarly, as mentioned in Chapter 3, a laser too can be used to direct team members for purposes of movement or target engagement. Combined with verbal communication (e.g., "My light beam is on the suspect" or "He's 30 meters away, at 2 o'clock from my laser spot"), a flashlight or laser can greatly enhance the clarity of such directions.

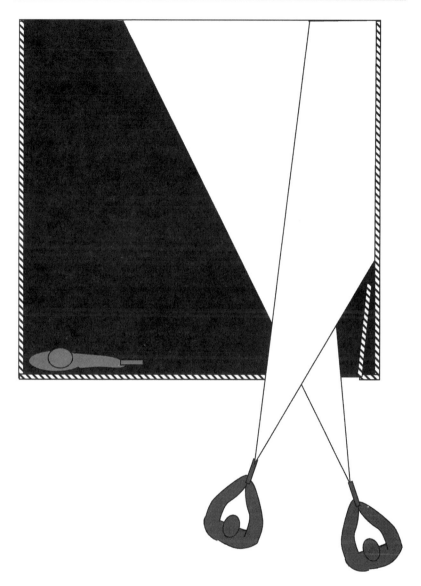

One possible answer to a low-light room entry problem. First clear and domi-nate the majority of the room with high-intensity beams, at some point verify-ing a clear path. Make entry with lights off, illuminating the remaining hard corner after penetration (p. 163–167).

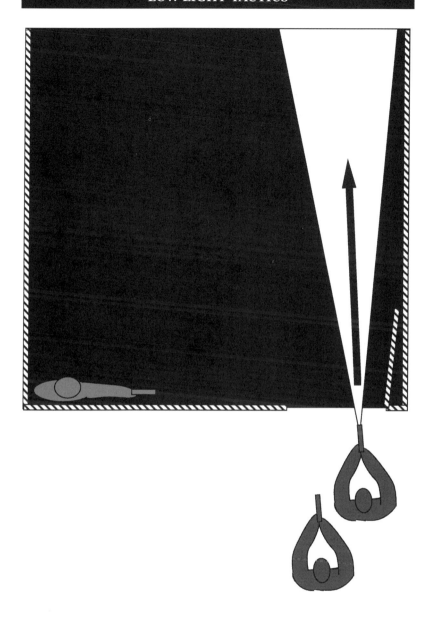

Coordinated movement to achieve a common goal is the final element of team tactics. Note that to maintain a cohesive team at night, the distance interval between members of a given maneuver element will usually have to be reduced compared with daytime operations; in extreme cases this means maintaining physical contact with each other. Resources must be brought to bear at the right time and place, placing the enemy under duress from a number of directions (but without crossfire). In the case of low-light operations, this can also involve coordinated illumination.

By randomly alternating which member uses illumination, a team can thoroughly confuse an adversary as to what is actually happening. The effect is much like fireflies in the darkness, and anyone observing the scene will have little idea of the actual number and location of his opponents.

One caution, however: when operating with one or more partners, you must pay attention to the effects of your light vis-à-vis the position of your team member(s) to prevent backlighting them. A rule of thumb to avoid this tactical faux pas is that only the front person in a given element should use his or her light, unless there is an overriding reason for others to supply illumination.

As a simple example of how tactical illumination can benefit a team, take the case of a two-person room entry as illustrated on pages 163–167. When you are entering any room, the primary problem is the "fatal funnel" delimited by the doorway. Your adversary knows you must pass through this channelized area, and hence his uncertainty about where to aim is eliminated. When there is plenty of ambient illumination, the best you can hope for is to cause some sort of diversion and traverse the threshold as quickly as you can.

In dim light, we can apply tactical illumination to increase our odds. First, clear and dominate all areas that can be seen from outside, using the beam from a hand-held or weapon-mounted light to systematically "clear" the majority of the room without entering it. Remember, however, illumination tools should be used in a manner that appears random to anyone inside. At this point the area next to the near wall will be the only unknown.

At some point in the process, the lead member checks that there is a clear path into the room by sweeping the beam from near to far along the ground. Just prior to entry, all lights are turned off, and then the lead member moves deep into the room in the darkness. The number-two man follows close behind, and as he breaks the threshold, shines his light into the previously uncleared deep corner(s). Now the lead member can use his light to clear as necessary. With practice, the whole process takes only a couple of seconds.

To see how this tactic works, let's look at the entry from the assailant's-eye view. A typical assailant will press tight against the wall in a deep corner on the same side as the door, aiming his weapon to shoot the first person through. (Remember, we have already cleared the rest of the room from the outside.)

With the dynamic entry technique above, the assailant will most likely track the silhouette of the quickly moving lead team member into the room. In the darkness, this presents a difficult shot at best, particularly with the lateral weapon movement required. In any case, the number-two man should be able to bring his weapon (and light) to bear on the assailant before the bad guy can shoot. No guarantees, but better than the same situation in medium to bright lighting conditions.

Yet another lighting tactic is for part of the team to create a "wall of light" effect that allows the rest to maneuver unseen. With a sufficient level of high-intensity illumination- e.g., multiple hand-held or weapon-mounted models or large spotlight(s)—you can not only eliminate an assailant's ability to see team members moving behind the light source, but also conceal those in front of and below it.

Since the beam is conical in shape, the light(s) should be held high, from behind cover when such is available. Those moving in front of the wall of light should stay low—perhaps even crawling, or "duck walking" in a squatting position—to stay out of the conical beam area as much as possible. You'll need to experiment with this technique to determine the exact boundaries of this cloaking effect.

And remember: whether you use an intermittent lighting technique, the "wall of light," or some combination of the two will depend on your specific situation, including the manpower and equipment resources available.

When the team has access to NVE, consider alternating members with night vision devices and those using the "naked eye." Each sensor has its advantages, as do different types of NVE. The use of IR laser aimers on all team firearms, even those carried by operators without NVE, will facilitate target acquisition by everyone, directed by team members equipped with NVE. Whatever system you use, be sure to have a backup in case of breakage.

One final aspect of team operations in low light is the greater confidence felt by individual members. As noted previously, humans are prone to experiencing increased anxiety in the darkness. The knowledge that one is not alone goes a long way toward mitigating this uneasiness.

Whether operating as a team member or by yourself, you'll need to respond quickly to a dynamic tactical or self-defense situation, performing the required actions without conscious thought whenever possible. The path to this level of skill includes plenty of task-specific training.

9

LOW-LIGHT
FIREARMS AND
FORCE-ON-FORCE
TRAINING

WHEN ALL IS SAID AND DONE, proficiency at low-light combatives depends more on the software than the hardware. Which is to say, the operator is more important than his or her equipment. Even if you can afford the finest low-light tools, learning to use those devices will require an additional investment of time and effort. The best gear in the world is useless if you are not adept at using it.

Since my major field of study is fighting with firearms—with an emphasis on mind-set and tactics—what follows is largely specific to that discipline. Once again, this chapter is not intended as a comprehensive syllabus for low-light training. It merely offers a few thoughts on how to proceed. After beginning the process you will undoubtedly come up with additional ideas specific to your situation.

LIVE-FIRE TRAINING

This may sound obvious, but the best low-light training is to actually train in low light. No kidding. Be that as it may, in my experience many armed professionals who work at night rarely, if ever, train or practice under conditions of reduced illumination. (A notable exception is military special operations personnel.)

One reason for this lack of low-light training is undoubtedly the various logistical issues that arise when instructors and students cannot see clearly. Training sessions conducted under conditions of reduced illumination generally proceed more slowly and involve an increased risk of accidents. Still, given the statistical likelihood of a confrontation in dim light, it's well worth the hassle.

If you have an indoor range, low-light firearms training can be conducted at any time; it's a simple matter of flipping a switch or turning a rheostat to create any desired level of illumination. The lights can be turned on for scoring targets and the like, although dark adaption will be lost.

With an outdoor facility, on the other hand, training sessions must be held sometime between dusk and dawn. Hence you can either stay up late or get up very early. In either case you will probably need to modify your standard training procedures to achieve an acceptable level of low-light range safety.

First of all, a thorough grounding in basic firearms safety is a nonnegotiable prerequisite to any firearms training, especially in darkness. Demonstrating exemplary muzzle control, maintaining a straight trigger finger at all times except while firing, and conscientiously keeping weapons holstered and/or slung while not in use are a good start. Note that these procedures are important during actual low-light operations as well: decreased vision coupled with a higher probability of unintentional discharges due to startle and "sympathy fire" demand the maximum possible margin for error.

Since neither the rangemaster nor the shooters can see in

the dark, it is imperative that all shooters be familiar with range procedures and directions. Because students will be highly dependent on verbal commands, consider using a PA system or bullhorn when working with large groups. Chemical light sticks can be used to mark firing points and/or trainees.

Eye and ear protection should be worn during all firearms training, day or night. In low light, you'll want shooting glasses with clear lenses; any tint at all will cut down on light transmission. Electronic hearing protection with a high-decibel cutoff comes in especially handy at night, and a good set of stereo shooting muffs can even be used operationally since they can be set to amplify ambient sounds.

If you are an instructor, the responsibility for mishap-free training falls largely on your shoulders. You must be absolutely certain that no one is downrange before you commence firing, a more difficult proposition in the dark. Have everyone on line use their flashlights to visually inspect the impact and target areas.

Likewise, verifying that the line is safe at night presents a particular problem, since visual confirmation is less certain. Short of checking every shooter individually, a reasonable approach is to have shooters holster, sling, and/or clear their weapons and then step back from the firing line. The instructor can then ask if all weapons are safe and shine a light along the firing line to ascertain that it is safe to go downrange.

When illumination is required for administrative purposes such as scoring, use a light with red filter to minimize impact on dark adaption. For some exercises—e.g., escorting a relative beginner through a shoot house—instructors may wish to maintain physical contact with the shooter to ensure that he or she does not point a loaded weapon in an unsafe direction. Holding onto the back of the student's belt is a good way to accomplish this.

The bottom line with respect to low-light range safety is that with the reduction in the ability to visually monitor the firing line, everyone present bears an increased responsibili-

173

ty for preventing accidents. Advanced live-fire exercises in low light involving movement or team tactics should only be attempted by the most proficient individuals.

The ultimate goal of any firearms training is the level of unconscious competence. That is to say, one can perform all required combat shooting tasks reflexively while under stress. Of particular importance at night is the ability to hit targets at close range using "muscle memory." This will allow you to employ your firearms successfully under low-light conditions in which you can identify your target but not see your sights.

The added stress and difficulty of night-firing is not conducive to teaching beginners. Even seasoned shooters will experience a degradation in their marksmanship ability in low light. Hence, basic marksmanship training should be performed during the daytime.

You will also have to perform all gunhandling manipulations in the dark. For instance, checking weapon condition will often have to be done by feel in low light, as follows. Open the action and use your index finger to confirm that there is ammunition in the chamber(s); with magazine-fed weapons, push on the uppermost cartridge to ensure that the gun is topped off. With a magazine that feeds from either side (e.g., MP5, M-16), you can check that the top round is under the opposite lip after operating the action.

Similarly, you will need the ability to reload and clear malfunctions without looking. For this reason, I recommend a "wide spectrum remedy" method—e.g., "Tap (magazine), Rack (action), Re-engage (threat)"—for dealing with stoppages, as opposed to an approach that requires you to diagnose the problem first. With the latter strategy you'll have to do your best Helen Keller impersonation to determine why the gun didn't go bang, a potentially time-consuming process in the dark.

Relying on gross motor skills becomes more important than ever when you can't see. Train in robust methods that hold up under stress. For instance, work the action after each reload, instead of the fine motor movement of hitting a bolt/slide release and/or performing a chamber check.

The upshot is that daytime skills should be well honed in preparation for any low-light firearms training. It's also not a bad idea to practice all low-light skills (e.g., flashlight techniques) under good lighting before trying them in the dark. The result will be increased range safety plus a higher level of shooter confidence.

With respect to specific low-light training drills, a good place to start is to shoot your standard course of fire under a variety of illumination conditions, in particular dim lighting in which muzzle flash becomes a factor. You can actually use the flash to your advantage, using the retinal imprint of the sights to correct for follow-up shots. But remember: unless you are in the military, positive threat identification will always be a prerequisite to gunfire.

Other means of low-light aiming include superimposing the silhouette of the back of your handgun over the target just below the desired point of impact. If you have practiced enough to know by feel when the sights are aligned, the bullet will strike where you want it.Additionally, under certain lighting conditions, you can align your sights against a light background and then move the weapon on target without changing this alignment to fire. Of course, tritium night sights eliminate the need for this type of aiming technique.

Next, try each of the handgun and flashlight techniques described in Chapter 6. Find the one that works best with your equipment and shooting style and use it as your primary method of using a hand-held flashlight with your handgun. If that technique requires a particular type of light or switch location you should also become facile at a method that allows you to use other types of equipment. For example, the Rogers/Sure-Fire technique can only be used with a small light with protruding rear switch, but the Harries technique will work with any flashlight.

When multiple shooters practice flashlight techniques on the range, maintain sufficient spacing between firing points so that spillover illumination does not light up adjacent targets. Or run just one shooter at a time. The target engagement procedure is: "WEAPON UP—LIGHT ON—SHOOT—ASSESS RESULTS—LIGHT OFF—MOVE LATERALLY." This can be followed up with a 360-degree threat scan with the light on, and then another lateral change of position after it is turned off. (With multiple shooters on line, one sideways step in a specified direction will reinforce "light and move" tactics with minimal risk of students tripping over one another.)

If you use a weapon-mounted light, adequate nighttime practice with this tool is in order. Make sure to exercise all available switching options in the dark until you are completely familiar with momentary, constant-on, and/or disable functions. And if you train with the same weapon during the day, take off the lamp assembly to prevent breaking the filament prior to an operation; Laser Products makes a screw-on cap to protect the threads when the lamp assembly is removed. Likewise, practice with any laser aimers, optical sights, and NVE you plan to employ.

Also shoot using vehicle illumination, including hazard warning flashers; this simulates defending yourself during a roadside emergency, e.g., changing a flat tire. Similarly, police officers should fire strings under rotating or flashing colored emergency lights, plus spotlights and takedown lights. The Santa Ana, CA, Police Department has even constructed a cut-down patrol car, complete with light bar, for their indoor range!

To practice such situations from the opposite end, inexpensive clip-on lamps located near the target can be directed uprange to simulate car headlights pointed toward the shooter. Height and number can be varied to represent large trucks, motorcycles, multiple vehicles, and so on. And a target "holding" a cheap alkaline flashlight can simulate an adversary so equipped.

Targets can be illuminated intermittently by a training partner with a flashlight, simulating threat identification by a transient light source such as a passing car. Shooters then shoot at the previously identified but now darkened target, firing with handgun or shoulder weapon from the holster, sling, or tactical ready position. This is a challenging test of hand-eye coordination and kinesthetic presentation ("muscle memory"). Even so, highly experienced shooters can achieve some pretty impressive hits in this manner. To make this drill even more difficult, move off the attack line before shooting.

Tactical teams should conduct low-light entries in a live-fire shooting house to experience the effects of gun smoke from multiple weapons indoors on the use of illumination tools. Likewise, military operators should practice firing under ambient dim light—muzzle flash can be simulated by a remotely activated light set behind a silhouette target with a hole cut in it—and shoot at targets lit up by parachute flares, plus perform combined arms exercises using their full-range of night-fighting options. The number of possible drills and exercises is limited only by your imagination.

Incidentally, the case law established by *Popow v. City of Margate, N.J.* (476 F. Supp. 1237, 1979)—a federal court case filed under Title 42, Section 1983, of the United States Civil Rights Act—states that a failure to conduct realistic firearms training, to specifically include low-light firing, can constitute negligence by the agency involved. Hence, it is imperative that all law-enforcement instructors provide sufficient opportunity for low-light training.

I recommend a minimum of one night qualification per year, which should include, at a minimum, shooting under reduced ambient illumination, practice at handgun flashlight techniques, and strings fired under vehicle lights, with at least one timed weapon reload somewhere in the course of fire. Low-light exercises that require threat identification and discretionary shooting are also critical. If you don't have access to an indoor range and can't shoot outdoors at night, DeSantis night simulator goggles can be used in a pinch but cannot really substitute for actual low-light firing. Sadly, few departments meet this standard, and some do no night firing at all.

FORCE-ON-FORCE DRILLS

As noted in the previous chapter, selection of the optimum low-light tactics for a given situation is largely dependent on lighting conditions. But a mere intellectual understanding of illumination will not do. Your brain is unlikely to perform a conscious analysis of relative light levels and deliberately choose an appropriate course of action when you are under stress, and at any rate, there usually won't be time. What is needed is the subconscious ability to adapt to the ambient illumination, moving and using low-light tools in an optimal fashion.

The best way to ingrain these responses is through force-on-force training using Simunition FX rounds or conventional paintballs with both hand-held and weapon-mounted lights. The pain penalty of being struck by these nonlethal projectiles drives home all lessons learned at a gut level. For example, students quickly learn that overuse of illumination can get them shot, and that it is imperative to move after extinguishing the light. As with all good instruction, force-on-force follows a logical progression of drills, each designed to impart the skills required to move on to the next level.

But before you commence, everyone should be thoroughly briefed with respect to safety procedures. Even though a paintball or bullet from a marking cartridge cannot kill you, these projectiles can easily blind. Suitable protective gear—goggles with facemask and throat and groin protection at a minimum—must be worn at all times. Face masks should be taken off only at the direction of an instructor, once everyone has set down their guns. Verbal and flashlight commands can be used to communicate—for instance, flashing twice to indicate that participants are ready to begin, or making a circle with the beam to gather the group in one location. All training weapons should be checked by instructors prior to beginning, and no live firearms should be permitted in the training area. In the dark it is all too easy for a modified Simunition FX gun to be confused with an unaltered weapon.

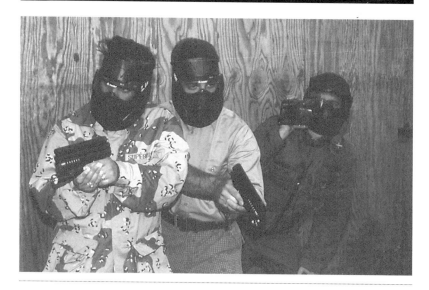

Force-on-force training in low light is the best way to gain an appreciation for the subtleties of self-supplied illumination tactics. (J.C. Ponce)

A good place to start your force-on-force training is with "gauntlet" drills, in which a single student will move with his or her weapon in an appropriate ready position through a corridor of wooden barricades. At selected intervals, live opponents step out—either armed aggressors who will fire at the student, or unarmed individuals who should not be shot. This Hogan's Alley with a pulse is only the first step, intended to teach the integration of movement and weapons handling.

Next, you should practice systematic, incremental, radial movement to view around the corners in a structure. Remember to illuminate in a manner that will appear random to your assailant. Cornering techniques comprise staple tools in the CQB operator's tactical toolbox. Seeing the environment in terms of angles—along with the ability to successfully negotiate these geometric obstacles—is the basis of a systematic and tactically sound method of clearing a structure.

To be a well-rounded operator, you will need the ability

to perform a combination of stealth and dynamic clearing methods; the exact techniques employed will vary depending on the specific floor plan in question. Some trainers recommend switching between right- and left-handed use of the firearm depending on the direction of the clearing process. This is done to minimize the amount of the shooter's body that is exposed as he or she rounds the corner.

There are some valid arguments against this procedure. For the average person I question the advisability of shooting from the "weak side" unless absolutely necessary, for instance, due to injury. Surgical shooting is required to stop real world adversaries, and most people don't even shoot that well from their dominant side. Sure, an extremely skilled shooter can become virtually ambidextrous, but only the exceptional individual will put in the trigger time to get this good. That said, if you are such a person, more power to you.

With a firm foundation of individual skills established, students can next learn to work in concert with others. Team drills should begin with two-on-two engagements that emphasize situational awareness and communication. The concept of "cross clearing" can be introduced at this point: engaging the flanks of a threat that is preoccupied by one's partner. Maintaining adequate distance from cover is critical to maximize tactical flexibility and avoid succumbing to a "Maginot Line" mentality and resulting false sense of security.

Four-on-ones come next: two pairs must coordinate to eliminate a single adversary. These drills reinforce the lessons learned in previous evolutions, while adding an additional level of complexity. Despite the odds, a lone aggressor *can* eliminate an uncoordinated team, as the FBI discovered during the tragic Miami shootout. The four-on-one exercises drive home the point that the maxim "individuals die, teams survive" only holds true when those who wear the same uniform coordinate sufficiently with their mates.

Upon completion of the above drills, students will have learned team fundamentals well enough that they can be formed into larger units. A variety of full-up scenarios can be presented, including simulated hostage situations, drug raids, barricaded suspects, and terrorist takeovers. All exercises should be videotaped when possible—though obviously this can be problematic in low light without specialized night-vision cameras—and a detailed debrief should be conducted immediately upon conclusion. Students should take turns as aggressors so that they may view the effects of lighting techniques and tactical errors from both sides.

One key principle in all team drills is that no one operates alone. A two-person element is the smallest unit of force employed and comprises a "team within a team." Multiple clearing elements can then be directed by the team leader to maximize the synergistic effect of all members. Note that team training should only be attempted once individual skills are sufficiently honed. Additionally, as with firearms training, it is a good idea to attain a basic prowess at daytime force-on-force before attempting the same drills in the dark.

Common errors to watch for include crowding cover, threat fixation, failure to keep the weapon in an appropriate ready position, leaving the light on too long, and failing to move once the light has been turned off. Team errors include lack of clear communication, erratic and uncoordinated movement, members operating solo, and failure to cover all likely threat axes.

Another common problem is fratricide, that is, so-called "friendly" fire. In conducting low-light force-on-force training, I have noticed a tendency for students to fire without positive threat ID in reduced illumination. This can occur either due to startle or as a result of "sympathy fire" when a teammate shoots—both phenomena are undoubtedly exacerbated by increased anxiety in the dark.

A good way to prevent such shooting at shadows is to include a roving bystander who is not to be shot in each skill-building exercise. Penalties (e.g., push-ups, forfeiting the bout, etc.) can then be assessed for hitting the bystander, or even for engaging any person without illuminating him first. Similarly, in full-up scenarios involving role-playing, the situation can be set up to maximize the probability that an innocent party will be shot by mistake. Making such mistakes in training will decrease the likelihood of a similar error on the street or in the field.

One nice thing about force-on-force drills and exercises is that they provide excellent "on-the-job training," facilitating self-evaluation and correction. Just be sure to follow your normal tactical procedures, fire discipline, cross-fire angles, and rules of engagement. And remember that real bullets can penetrate "cover" that will stop paintballs. Never allow your force-on-force training to degrade into a game, and remember that every paint projectile in the air is a surrogate for a metal bullet that could kill you, a teammate, or a bystander.

PROFESSIONAL INSTRUCTION

The quickest route to combat prowess is formal instruction. If you are in the military, avail yourself of any and all opportunities to increase your proficiency. In particular, pick the brains of any special operations forces in your area. These units tend to receive more and better training than run-of-the-mill troops, and often operate at night to minimize the probability of detection. Similarly, snipers can assist you with learning the art of stealthy movement.

As of this writing, live-fire firearms classes comprise the most common low-light training for civilians. Most private sector schools (e.g., Gunsite, Thunder Ranch, etc.) have a token "night shoot" during which students fire during dim-light and/or while using hand-held flashlight techniques. This is good as far as it goes, but given the fact that low-light confrontations are statistically the rule rather than the exception, you should partake of much more training in reduced illumination.

Some schools now offer specific night-shooting courses. Heckler & Koch International Training Division, the Smith & Wesson Academy, and SigArms Academy are three that come immediately to mind. Again the emphasis is on live-fire, albeit far more of it than conducted in a general combat-shooting course. Most people can use all the practice they can get, daytime or low-light, so spending a few days of quality trigger time never hurts.

The Smith & Wesson Academy low-light class also includes interactive role-playing scenarios with Simunition FX marking cartridges, and they offer a night-vision class for law enforcement as well. ITT, too, teaches a night-vision course, though it provides more of a general equipment overview than specifics on how to fight in the dark.

In contrast to shooting-range classes, the Sure-Fire Institute and Combative Concepts, Inc., focus primarily on force-on-force-type training. As noted in the preceding section, this type of nonlethal gunfight simulation provides tactical benefits far beyond low-light marksmanship and gun-handling skills. Classes are offered either at the SFI "Battle Lab" or off site. As of this writing, longtime CCI personnel are the primary instructors for SFI. They developed most of the illumination tactics described in the previous chapter, plus the above paintball drills. For law enforcement personnel and military teams, SFI/CCI training is hard to beat; private citizens, too, can benefit as long as they keep in mind that their self-defense goals will often be quite different.

If your agency or organization conducts force-on-force training in house, I strongly recommend that the instructional staff attend Ken Murray's use-of-force simulations instructor course through Armiger Police Training Institute. A pioneer in the industry, Ken is one of the founders of Simunitions, and his course can save you time and money, make your training much more effective, and (most importantly) prevent death or injury due to preventable training accidents, reducing potential liability in the process.

Last but not least, my company (Options for Personal Security, OPS for short) can provide state-of-the-art low-light instruction, including both live-fire and force-on-force classes. You can either take a scheduled OPS course on site in California, Florida, or Texas, or contract for a mobile training team to come to your area and conduct a class. The curriculum can be tailored to meet your mission-essential requirements.

183

IN CONCLUSION

THE BEST PARTING ADVICE I can offer is to make a realistic appraisal of your needs, procure any necessary low-light tools, and then study and train as much as you can. Take as many applicable courses as possible from qualified instructors who focus on defensive and/or tactical application. No one person has all the answers, regardless of what he or she may claim.

Then practice diligently until you can perform the required tasks consistently, under stress, in the dark. In the words of the U.S. Navy SEALs, paraphrasing General George S. Patton quoting the Roman Legion, "Train hard, fight easy." There are no shortcuts to proficiency, and never have been.

The field of low-light combatives is evolving even as you read this. Inevitably, I'll have learned additional techniques, tactics, and training exercises since this book has gone to press that would have been included in the appropriate chapters. Equipment, too, will evolve. You'll have to discover these things on your own, using the information found herein as a foundation. Good luck in your continuing quest for knowledge and skill, and stay as safe as your situation allows.

RESOURCE GUIDE

LOW-LIGHT TRAINING

Options for Personal Security (author)
P.O. Box 489
Sebring, FL 33871-0489

Sure-Fire Institute
18310 Mt. Washington
Fountain Valley, CA 92708

Combative Concepts, Inc.
826 Orange Ave. #518
Coronado, CA 92118

Smith & Wesson Academy
2100 Roosevelt Ave.
Springflield, MA 01101

Heckler & Koch International Training Division
21480 Pacific Blvd.
Sterling, VA 22170-8903

SigArms Academy
Corporate Park
Exeter, NH 03833

Armiger Police Training Institute
P.O. Box 877
Gotha, FL 33734

Dr. Paul Michel (low-light vision consultant)
31461 Island Dr.
Evergreen, CO 80439

LOW-LIGHT TOOLS

Laser Products (Sure-Fire lights)
18300 Mt. Baldy Circle
Fountain Valley, CA 92708

Streamlight, Inc.
1030 W. Germantown Pike
Norristown, PA 19403

Mag Instruments, Inc.
1635 S. Sacramento Ave.
Ontario, CA 91761

Sage International
630 Oakland Ave.
Pontiac, MI 48342

Insight Technologies
3 Technology Drive
Londonderry, NH 03053

Wilcox Industries, Corp.
53 Durham St.
Portsmouth, NH 03801

GO-Light
Rt. 61 Box 40
Hayes Center, NE 69032

Patrol Bike Systems (bicycle lights)
P.O. Box 9308
St. Paul, MN 55109-9308

Diamond Products Marketing, Inc. (light mounts)
2300 Commerce Park Dr.#6
Palm Bay, FL 32905

Tac Star Industries
P.O. Box 70
Cottonwood, AZ 86326

Armament Systems and Products (ASP)
P.O. Box 1794
Appleton, WI 54913

Crimson Trace
1433 N.W. Quimby St.
Portland, OR 97209

Lasermax
3495 Winton Place, Bldg. B
Rochester, NY 14623

Excalibur Enterprises (Night Vision Equipment Corporation)
P.O. Box 400
Fogelsville, PA 18051-0400

ITT Night Vision
7671 Enon Drive
Roanoke, VA 24019

Aimpoint
420 W. Main St.
Geneseo, IL 61254

Trijicon
P.O. Box 930059
Wixom, MI 48393-0059

Ashley Outdoors
2401 Ludelle
Fort Worth, TX 76105

Hesco/Meprolight
2139 Greenville Rd.
LaGrange, GA 30241

Innovative Weaponry, Inc. (PT Night Sights)
2513 E. Loop 820 N.
Ft. Worth, TX 76118

Dillon Precision (Smith Vortex Flash Suppressor)
8009 E. Dillon's Way
Scottsdale, AZ 85260

Knights Armaments Corporation
7750 9th Street S.W.
Vero Beach, FL 32968

Safariland, Ltd.
3120 E. Mission Blvd.
Ontario, CA 91761

Eagle Industries
400 Biltmore Drive, Suite 530B
Fenton, MO 63026

Blade Tech
360 S. 96th St.
Tacoma, WA 98409

Gemtech
P.O. Box 3538
Boise, ID 83703-0538

AWC
P.O. Box 41938
Phoenix, AZ 85080-1938

Cold Steel
2128-D Knoll Dr.
Ventura, CA 93003

Emerson Knives, Inc.
P.O. Box 4325
Redondo Beach, CA 90278-9998

Benchmade
300 Beavercreek Rd.
Oregon City, OR 97045

Spyderco
P.O. Box 800
Golden, CO 80402-0800

Allen Elishewitz
17194 Preston Rd.
Suite 123 #227
Dallas, TX 75248-1203

Bud Neally
822 Thomas St.
Stroudsburg, PA 18360

Ontario Knives
P.O. Box 145
Franklinville, NY 14737

James Piorek
P.O. Box 5032
Missoula, MT 59806

Round Eye Knife and Tool
P.O. Box 818
Sagle, ID 83860

B-Safe Industries (protective apparel)
P.O. Box 153-H
Scarsdale, NY 10583-8653

RECOMMENDED READING

The Night Fighter's Handbook, **by Maj. Dennis J. Popp**
Primarily intended for use by military units, this book contains a lot of good information on nighttime land navigation.

Laser Sights and Night Vision Devices, **by Duncan Long**
Basically a catalog of low-light tools. Contains several technical errors, but still worth reading.

Defensive Tactics with Flashlights, **by John Peters**
Simple, effective techniques for use with the full-sized "police" flashlight. Also contains legal citations for a number of flashlight use-of-force cases.

Predator Training, **by Greg Jones**
This excellent book on the mental aspects of the martial art Kung Fu San Soo contains a good chapter on low light hand-to-hand combat.

ITT NIGHT VISION SELECTION GUIDE

The following glossary originally appeared in an ITT night vision brochure for law enforcement. It only contains a few explicit plugs for ITT equipment—good gear in any case—and the content is factually accurate.

ITT Night Vision Terminology

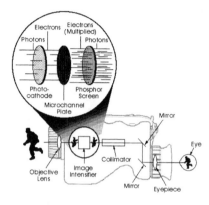

How Night Vision Works

In Generation 2 and 3 systems, the objective lens collects light that you cannot see with your naked eye and focuses it on the image intensifier. Inside the image intensifier a photocathode absorbs this light energy and converts it into electrons. These electrons are then drawn toward a phosphor screen but first pass through a microchannel plate that multiplies them thousands of times. When this highly intensified electron image strikes the phosphor screen, it causes the screen to emit light that you can see. Since the phosphor screen emits this light in exactly the same pattern and degrees of intensity as the light that is collected by the objective lens, the bright nighttime image you see in the eyepiece corresponds precisely to the outside scene you are viewing.

Terminology

Automatic Brightness Control (ABC) — An electronic feature that automatically reduces voltages to the microchannel plate to keep the image intensifier's brightness within optimal limits and protects the tube. The effect of this can be seen when rapidly changing from low-light to high-light conditions; the image gets brighter and then, after a momentary delay, suddenly dims to a constant level.

Black Spots — These are cosmetic blemishes in the image intensifier or can be dirt or debris between the lenses. Black spots that are in the image intensifier do not affect the performance or reliability of a night vision device and some number of varying size are inherent in the manufacturing processes. Spots due to dirt or debris between the lenses should be removed by careful cleaning if the system is designed for interchanging optics.

Bright-Source Protection (BSP): An electronic function that reduces the voltage to the photocathode when the night vision device is exposed to bright light sources such as room lights or car lights. BSP protects the image tube from damage and enhances its life; however, it also has the effect of lowering resolution when functioning.

Cycles per Milliradian (cy/mr): Units used to measure system resolution. A milliradian is the angle created by 1 yard at a distance of 1,000 yards. This means that a device that can detect two 1/2-yard objects separated by 1/2 yard at 1,000 yards has a resolution of 1.0 cy/mr. Do not confuse cy/mr with line pair per millimeter. For example, a system can have a 3X lens attached and increase the system resolution by a factor of 3, yet the image intensifier's resolution (measured in lp/mm) has not increased.

Diopter : The unit of measure used to define eye correction or the refractive power of a lens. Usually adjustments to an optical eyepiece accommodates for differences in individual eyesight. Many military systems provide a +2 to -6 diopter range.

Distortion (above right): Three types of distortion are most significant to night vision devices: geometric, "S", and shear. **Geometric distortion:** is inherent in all Gen 0 and Gen I image intensifiers and in some Gen 2 image intensifiers that use electrostatic rather than fiber-optic inversion of the image. Geometric distortion is eliminated in image tubes that use a microchannel plate and fiber optics for image inversion; however, some S-distortion can occur in these tubes

194

NORMAL

GEOMETRIC

GEOMETRIC

"S"

SHEAR

Non-inverting image intensifiers that use microchannel plates and clear glass for the optics are free of distortion. The image intensifier ITT manufactures for its Night Enforcer is distortion free.

S-distortion: results from the twisting operation in manufacturing fiber-optic inverters. Usually S-distortion is very small and is difficult to detect with the unaided eye. Gen 2 image tubes manufactured to U.S. military standards since 1988 have nearly no perceptible S-distortion. **Shear distortion:** can occur in any image tube that uses fiber-optic bundles for the phosphor screen. It appears as a cleavage or dislocation in a straight line viewed in the image area; as though the line were "sheered."

Equivalent Background Illumination (EBI): This is the amount of light you see in an image tube that is turned on but there is no light at all on the photocathode; it is affected by temperature where the warmer the night vision device, the brighter the background illumination. EBI is measured in lumens per square centimeter (lm/cm2) wherein the lower the value the better. The EBI level determines the lowest light level at which you can detect something and below this light level, objects will be masked by the EBI.

Emission Point: A steady or fluctuating pinpoint of bright light in the image area that does not go away when all light is blocked from the objective lens. The position of an emission point within the field of view will not move. If an emission point disappears or is only faintly visible when viewing under brighter nighttime conditions, it is not indicative of a problem. If the emission point remains bright under all lighting conditions, the system needs to be repaired. Do not confuse an emission point with a point light source in the scene being viewed.

Eye Relief: The distance your eyes must be from the last element of an eyepiece in order to achieve the optimal image area.

Fixed-Pattern Noise (FPN) (left): A faint hexagonal (honeycomb) pattern throughout the image area that most often occurs under high-light conditions. This pattern is inherent in the structure of the microchannel plate and can be seen in virtually all Gen 2 and Gen 3 systems if the light level is high enough.

Footlambert (fL): A unit of brightness equal to one footcandle at a distance of one foot.

Gain: Also called brightness gain or luminance gain. This is the number of times a night vision device amplifies light input. It is usually measured as tube gain and system gain. Tube gain is measured as the light output (in fL) divided by the light input (in fc). This figure is usually seen in values of tens of thousands. If tube gain is pushed too high, the tube will be "noisier" and the signal-to-noise ratio may go down. U.S. military Gen 2 and Gen 3 image tubes operate at gains of between 20,000 and 37,000. On the other hand, system gain is measured as the light output (fL) divided by the light input (also fL) and is what the user actually sees. System gain is usually seen in the thousands. U.S. military systems operate at 2,000 to 3,000. In any night vision system, the tube gain is reduced by the system's lenses and is affected by the quality of the optics or any filters; therefore, system gain is a more important measurement to the user.

Gallium Arsenide (GaAs): The semiconductor material used in manufacturing the Gen 3 photocathode. GaAs photocathodes have a very high photosensitivity in the spectral region of about 450 to 950 nanometers (visible and near-infrared region).

Generation 0: Typically uses an S-1 photocathode with peak response in the blue-green region (with a photosensitivity of 60 µA/lm), electrostatic inversion, and electron acceleration to achieve gain. Consequently, Gen 0 tubes are characterized by the presence of geometric distortion and the need for active infrared illumination.

Generation 1: Typically uses an S-20 photocathode (with photosensitivity of 180-200 µA/lm), electrostatic inversion, and electron acceleration to achieve gain. Because of higher photosensitivity, Gen 1 was the first truly passive image intensifier. Gen1 is characterized by geometric distortion, performance at low light levels, and blooming.

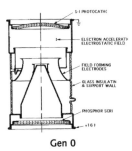

Gen 0

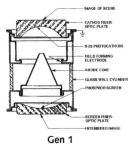

Gen 1

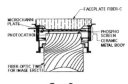

Gen 2

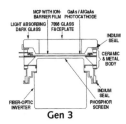

Gen 3

Generation 2: Usually an S-25 (extended red) photocathode (with photosensitivity of 240+ μA/lm and a microchannel plate to achieve gain. Can be found with either electrostatic or fiber-optic inversion. Gen 2 tubes provide satisfactory performance at low light levels and exhibit low distortion.

Generation 3: Uses gallium-arsenide for the photocathode and a microchannel plate for gain. The microchannel plate is also coated with an ion barrier film to increase tube life. Produces more than 800 μA/lm in the 450 to 950 nanometer (near-infrared) region of the spectrum. Gen 3 provides very good to excellent low-light-level performance, long tube life. Recent mil-spec quality tubes have no perceptible distortion.

Line Pairs per Millimeter (lp/mm): Units used to measure image intensifier resolution. Usually determined from a 1951 Air Force Resolving Power Test Target. The target is a series of different sized patterns composed of three horizontal and three vertical lines. You must be able to distinguish all the horizontal and vertical lines and the spaces between them to qualify for that pattern.

Lumen: The unit denoting the photons perceivable by the human eye in one second.

Microamps per Lumen (μA/lm): The measure of electrical current (μA) produced by a photocathode when it is exposed to a measured amount of light (lumens).

Microchannel Plate (MCP): A metal-coated glass disk that multiplies the electrons produced by the photocathode. An MCP is found only in Gen 2 and Gen 3 systems. These devices normally have anywhere from 2 to 6 million holes (or channels) in them. Electrons entering a channel strike the wall and knock off additional electrons which in turn knock off more electrons producing a cascading effect. MCPs eliminate the distortion characteristic of Gen 0 and Gen I systems. The number of holes in an MCP is a major factor in determining resolution. ITT's new MCPs have 6.34 million holes or channels compared to the previous standard of 3.14 million.

Milliamps per Watt (mA/W): The measure of electrical current (mA) produced by a photocathode when exposed to a specified wavelength of light at a given radiant power (watt). As with microamps per lumen, usually, the higher the value, the better the performance; however, it is important to know where in the spectrum the wavelength falls. Because more night light is present in the near-infrared region than in the visible or ultraviolet regions, a high value in the blue regions would not be a good as a moderate value in the near-infrared region.

Near-Infrared: The shortest wavelengths of the infrared region, nominally 750 to 2,500 nanometers. Gen 2 operates from around 450 to 950 nanometers.

Photocathode: The input surface of an image intensifier that absorbs light energy and in turn releases electrical energy in the form of an electron image. The type of material used is a distinguishing characteristic of the different generations of image intensifiers.

Photoresponse (PR): See Photosensitivity.

Photosensitivity: Also called photocathode sensitivity. The ability of the photocathode material to produce an electrical response when subjected to light waves (photons). Usually measured in microamps of current per lumen of light (μA/lm). The higher the value, the better the ability to produce a visible image under darker conditions.

Resolution: The ability of an image intensifier or night vision system to distinguish between objects close together. Image intensifier resolution is measured in line pairs per millimeter (lp/mm) while system resolution is measured in cycles per milliradian. For any particular night vision system, the image intensifier resolution will remain constant while the system resolution can be affected by altering the objective or eyepiece optics by adding magnification or relay lenses. Often the resolution in the same night vision device is very different when measured at the center of the image and at the periphery of the image. This is especially important for devices selected for photography or video where the entire image resolution is important.

Signal-to-Noise Ratio (SNR): A measure of the light signal reaching the eye divided by the perceived noise as seen by the eye. A tube's SNR determines the low-light-resolution of the image tube; therefore, the higher the SNR, the better the ability of the tube to resolve objects with good contrast under low-light conditions. Because SNR is directly related to the photocathode's sensitivity and also accounts for phosphor efficiency and MCP operating voltage, it is the best single indicator of an image intensifier's performance.

Scintillation: A faint, random, sparkling effect throughout the image area. Scintillation is a normal characteristic of microchannel plate image intensifiers and is more pronounced under low-light-level conditions. Sometimes called "video noise." Do not confuse scintillation with emission points.

Spectrum: The range of electromagnetic energy from cosmic rays to extra-low frequency used in submersed submarine communication.

NOTE: Electromagnetic frequency is measured in cycle per second and wavelength in microns or nanometers. The ultraviolet region extends from 100 to 400 nm with the near-ultraviolet nominally 300 to 400 nm. The visible portion of the spectrum extends from 400 to 750 nm. The infrared region extends from 750 to 2x105 nm with the near-infrared nominally 750 to 2,500 nm.

Evaluation of NV Equipment

Characteristics of night vision equipment fall into four major categories that help in evaluation: performance, human factors, suitability to its application, and the overall cost of ownership. If you have any questions, do not hesitate to call ITT

Performance: The very need for a night vision capability necessarily focuses on performance as the most important — Can you see a clear image when it is dark and you cannot see the scene or objects with your unaided eye? Most night vision equipment available today will provide an adequate image under higher night light conditions such as a full moon. Evaluate the following parameters to determine how well a system will perform when you need to see under truly dark conditions such as starlight.

Photosensitivity: The ability of a night vision system to detect light energy and convert it to an electron image is reflected in the image intensifier's photosensitivity. Usually, the higher the value, the better the ability to "see" under darker and darker conditions. However, be aware that at night there is more light energy available in the near-infrared region than in the visible region. Therefore, if a device claims a high photosensitivity, make sure to find out where in the spectrum this is measured. A high photosensitivity in the blue or visible region may not perform as well as another system with a lower overall photosensitivity, but a higher value in the near-infrared region.

Signal-to-Noise Ratio (SNR): This is probably the single most significant factor in determining a system's ability to see when it gets dark. Be aware that SNR can be computed many ways to get desired results. Be sure to find out how SNR was computed. When measured according to U.S. mil specs, the SNR takes into account the photosensitivity, as well as the efficiency of the phosphor screen in reconverting the electron image to visible light and the "noise" contribution of the microchannel plate. Because the SNR determines an image intensifier's low-light-resolution, the higher the ratio, the clearer will be the signal compared to the background noise, hence, the better the ability to see under increasingly darker conditions.

Gain: This tends to be a confusing parameter when evaluating night vision devices. The most important gain measurement is the system gain. Very high gain values for an image tube are not especially significant — the U.S. military procures devices with the tube gain ranging from 20,000 to 37,000. Look for the system gain. U.S. military systems operate at 2,000 to 3,000. The higher the value the better the ability of the device to amplify the light it detects. A word of caution; gain is only part of the story. If a system does not possess a good photosensitivity and SNR, a very high gain value simply means that you will make a poor image brighter, not better.

Also, very high gain values could mean the tube is driven very hard and the life of the tube will be reduced. The very best test is field evaluation under very dark conditions.

Resolution: Usually this is measured as tube resolution (lp/mm) or system resolution (cy/mr). The more significant measurement is system resolution as this is what the viewer will actually experience and takes into account the quality of the system's optics. If you are evaluating systems with similar optical quality and filters, the tube resolution is an important criteria. Resolution is often measured at high- and low-light conditions. Most systems produce an optimal resolution at some point between very high light and very low light conditions. As long as resolution is measured the same way using the same magnification and the same conditions (i.e., per U.S. mil specs) the higher the value, the better the ability to present a sharp picture. However, be aware that many devices will produce a sharp image in the center of the viewing area, but not as sharp as you look toward the periphery. The lack of a sharp image, except at the center of the viewing area, can be due to the presence of a Gen 0 image tube or to the system's optics. Again, remember that many night vision systems will produce adequate results under higher night-light conditions, but perform poorly under darker conditions.

Human Factors: Here, such issues as weight, size, safe equipment, and the ease of operation should be considered. Remember that the ease of operation should be determined under dark conditions where the user cannot see the device being used. What may appear to be an acceptable level of operating ease under room lights may not be "user friendly" at all when it is dark. Protracted use should also be considered when evaluating weight. What may seem an acceptable weight when using a device for a short time, may not be so when viewing for long periods of time. Additionally, consider such functions as the on/power switch. Will you need to continually hold down the switch? – even light pressure for one finger for a long time can produce fatigue. Do you need to repeatedly press the switch to recharge the image tube? – such devices usually produce an initially bright image which gradually fades, reducing the ability to see and then shuts off unless you repress the switch. This characteristic could cause you to lose an image at a crucial moment.

Suitability to its Application: Within this category, characteristics such as field of view (FOV), magnification, versatility, weather resistance, and image distortion affect the ability of a night vision device to perform as needed.

Magnification and FOV: Regarding magnification and FOV, consider the distance you will need and the overall area you are observing or searching. For most surveillance or search applications, the higher the magnification or narrower the FOV, the greater the number of times you need to scan an area to avoid missing important objects or events. Usually a 1:1 lens with a 40° FOV provides optimal performance. For long range observation or weaponsight applications, the amount of magnification needed will vary; however, be sure to consider the other performance characteristics of the device; as the magnification increases, FOV decreases and the F number increases, all reducing the amount of light captured. Consequently, you will need an image tube with excellent performance at very low-light levels and/or high-performance lenses. Another factor involves the versatility of a device if it is used in situations that may require different magnification. How easily and quickly can the magnification be changed? Is it necessary to open the system to install the optics? In some cases, this may be inescapable, and the susceptibility of internal components to damage should be considered.

Distortion: Gen 0, Gen 1, and 25-mm Gen 2 electrostatically inverted image tubes produce a certain amount of geometric distortion in the image. In Gen 3 and 18-mm Gen 2 systems, geometric distortion is eliminated although it is possible to encounter some perceptible S- and shear distortion. The degree of any distortion and its interference with the application should be considered. When the application involves photography, video work, or weaponsights, the distortion and peripheral resolution are critical.

Weather Resistance: The ability of a night vision system to operate under adverse environmental conditions is another important factor. Any system built to U.S. mil specs for environmental factors will perform suitably under almost any condition encountered. The major concern is internal fogging that destroys the ability to see an image, hence, the ability to resist humidity and moisture is vital. In addition, when a night vision system is used on or around rivers or bodies of water, floatability can be a determining factor. ITT's Night Enforcer 150 monocular and 250 binocular will float if dropped into water.

Overall Cost of Ownership: Evaluation factors that impact the actual cost of acquiring a night vision capability are image tube life (referred to as "reliability"), warranty coverage, repair availability, service support, and overall workmanship as an indicator of quality. When evaluating night vision equipment, the initial acquisition cost does not equate to the cost of ownership. How often will you need a new image tube? What is the likelihood for repairs?

Are batteries available? What about exposure to bright lights? All image intensifiers will "wear out" over time due to gases generated within the tube that migrate to the photocathode and slowly kill it. Because of this, characteristics such as reliability, a bright-source protection (BSP) circuit, and the presence or absence of an ion-barrier film on the microchannel plate are important. U.S. mil specs describe procedures for projecting reliability. You should know what the reliability is for the tube you evaluate.

An important factor that can influence reliability is the voltage used to produce gain. If an image tube is "driven" hard to produce high gain, it will accelerate the production of gases and more quickly kill the ability to convert light into electrons. A final evaluation criteria is to determine whether or not the night vision device incorporates automatic protection for the image intensifier when it is exposed to high-light conditions or bright-light sources. Image tubes manufactured by ITT have a BSP circuit built into the image intensifier. This circuit automatically reduces the voltage to the photocathode when the system is exposed to bright light sources. The BSP feature protects the image tube and enhances its life. If there is doubt, consult the warranty; does it exclude exposure to high light or bright lights?

Note 1: Generation classification: Some night vision advertising has presented confusing information listing Russian equipment as Gen 1, Gen 2, and Gen 3, when in fact, by worldwide classification it is Gen 0, Gen I, and Gen 2, respectively.

Note 2: Reconditioned Generation 2: While the prices of "reconditioned Gen 2 systems may be attractive, be aware that the hours of remaining life and photosensitivity performance cannot be restored to Gen 2 tubes. "Reconditioned" usually means the system has a new or repaired power supply but the photosensitivity will be lower, the SNR will be lower, and the remaining life will be less. Some reconditioned units may be operating at below acceptable minimums and few companies possess the necessary test equipment to evaluate the tube's level of performance. The U.S. military specifications for Gen 2 require a reliability of 2,000 hours of operating time (ITT's new Gen 2 image intensifier has tested to well beyond the military specification). This situation does not pertain to Gen 3 equipment. Due to the presence of an ion-barrier film in Gen 3 devices, the gallium-arsenide photocathode is protected from degradation and the life and performance are extended many times longer than Gen 2.

CARE AND FEEDING OF Ni-Cd BATTERIES

The following is an internal Laser Products memo from research and development engineer Dr. Peter Hauk to company president Dr. John Matthews. If you wonder about the nitty gritty details of why you shouldn't fully discharge your rechargeable batteries, this should answer your questions.

Date: January 4, 1994
To: J.W. Matthews, et.al.
From: P. Hauk
Re: Care and Use of Ni-Cd Flashlight Batteries

• Overdischarging
Ni-Cd batteries are made up of individual cells connected end-to-end "in series." (The popular use of the term "battery" to describe both an individual cell and a multi-cell battery is not used here.) In a new battery all the cells will be closely matched in electrical capacity

and during use all the cells will become exhausted at nearly the same time. If one of the cells has a reduced capacity, then during use it will become exhausted before the other normal cells. When this happens, continued use will allow the normal cells to force current through the "weak" cell. Since this current is in the opposite direction of the current used during cell recharging, this process is referred to as "reverse charging." While standard recharging undoes the chemical changes that occur during battery cell use, reverse charging decomposes water within the cell into oxygen and hydrogen gasses. With continued reverse charging, pressure from these gasses increases until, at several PSI, the cell starts venting oxygen and hydrogen into the battery compartment. This venting damages the cell and reduces its capacity even more. It is also possible for such a gas mixture to be ignited by a spark and burn rapidly, generating both heat and pressure, which will damage the battery and other flashlight components.

To minimize any risk from this process, Sure-Fire flashlight models using Ni-Cd batteries now incorporate a venting device which prevents the build-up of gas pressure in the battery compartment. Moreover there is a very simple precaution which can eliminate any reverse charging.

The exhaustion of even one cell in a typical Ni-Cd flashlight battery will cause an abrupt and very noticeable reduction in the light output. The user is assured of safe operation and best battery lifetime by discontinuing operation and recharging the battery when this change occurs.

• **Underdischarging and "Memory Effect"**

There has been much written about the so-called "memory effect" in Ni-Cd batteries. It is argued that repeated partial discharge of Ni-Cd batteries results in a significantly reduced capacity. It has also been proposed that periodic complete discharging of a battery will "recondition" the battery and eliminate this "memory effect." While it is true that even modern premium Ni-Cd batteries will exhibit a temporarily reduced capacity after extended storage at elevated temperatures, they do not exhibit any noticeable "memory effect." More importantly, a complete "reconditioning" discharge risks reverse charging one or more battery cells and permanent battery damage (see above). Again, in normal use, the best policy is to recharge the flashlight battery when the light dims significantly.

• Recharging and Overcharging

Ni-Cd battery cells are recharged by forcing current through them so as to restore the electrochemical energy expended during discharge. This process varies in efficiency from about 65 percent at lower recharge currents to over 90 percent at high currents.

During the early stages of recharge the most accessible or most active sites on the electrodes undergo electrochemical recharge conversion at relatively low recharge voltages. As recharge continues, less accessible or less active sites are converted at increasingly higher recharge voltages. As the recharge voltage increases, another chemical reaction cycle begins to compete with electrode conversion for the recharge current: oxygen gas is electrochemically generated at the positive electrode. At higher conversion rates these ion concentrations are lower at the electrodes and the oxygen cycle is less important. This explains the greater recharge efficiency at higher recharge currents. As the battery cell becomes fully recharged, the rates of the electrode conversion reactions decrease, the electrolyte ion concentrations at the electrodes increase, and, consequently, the oxygen cycle rate increases. Since the oxygen cycle is now facilitated by higher electrolyte force this reaction decreases. It is this voltage decrease that is exploited by so-called "negative delta V" recharging circuits which discontinue high-rate recharging at this point.

Continued "recharging" (actually overcharging) simply drives the oxygen cycle, heats the battery cells, and elevates the internal cell pressure. While premium rapid-charge Ni-Cd battery cells have specially improved negative electrodes with increased gas absorption characteristics which limit oxygen cycle pressure build-up, oxygen cycle overheating at high currents can permanently damage battery cells. Thus all high current (rapid-charge) battery chargers require some means of determining recharge completion in order to avoid cell overheating. Since charged Ni-Cd battery cells slowly discharge through internal current leakage paths, particularly at elevated temperatures, some recharging devices provide for a small "maintenance current to keep the battery fully charged. Any maintenance current not used for electrode conversion reactions goes to drive the oxygen cycle at a low, safe rate.

At low recharge temperatures, both the electrode conversion and oxygen cycle reactions are inhibited. At very low temperatures (below 10° C, 50° F), the recharge voltage may rise high enough to start dissociation of water in the electrolyte, generating hydrogen and oxygen gasses. The hydrogen gas pressure in the battery cells may cause venting of hydrogen into the battery compartment and pose the same risks associated with "reverse" charging. The recommended temperature ranges for recharging are:

Standard charge (< 10 hr.):
       0° to 45° C (32° to 113° F)
Rapid charge (1 to 2 hr.):
       10° to 45°C (50° to 104° F)

CARE AND FEEDING OF Ni-Cd BATTERIES

Since cell service life will be shortened if recharging is always done at the low or high end of these temperature ranges, recharging should be done at 20° to 30° C (68° to 86° F).

• **Undercharging**

Even in a battery with cells well matched for capacity there may be differences between cells in recharge efficiency. Among similar cells there is no direct correlation between capacity and recharge efficiency. Therefore, as a battery is recharged, some cells may finish recharging while others are not fully recharged, particularly at lower recharge temperatures. If recharging is stopped at this time and the battery put into flashlight service, the useable run-time will be shortened. It is best to completely recharge the battery before use.

• **Summary**

There are three simple rules for rechargeable Ni-Cd flashlight battery care which will insure maximum utility and longest service life:

1. During use, when the light output first decreases noticeably, turn off the flashlight and recharge the battery.
2. Fully recharge, but do not overcharge the battery.
3. Recharge the battery at room temperature: 20° to 30° C (68° to 86° F).

205